THE
GRIND
LINE

Photo courtesy of Dave Coulier

THE GRIND LINE

The gears that powered the Detroit Red Wings to the summit

KEITH GAVE

Cover design: Josh Chamberlain

ISBN: 979-8-218-49937-2

First Edition

Printed and published in the United States of America.

Visit our website at: www.keithgaveauthor.com
Contact the author at: keith@keithgaveauthor.com

This book is available in quantity at special discounts for your group or organization. For further information, or to contact the author for special appearances, contact: media@keithgaveauthor.com

Teufelsberg Productions
PO Box 131
Houghton Lake Heights, Michigan 48630

On the cover: Players pictured, from left: Joe Kocur, Darren McCarty, Kris Draper and Kirk Maltby

Also by Keith Gave

The Russian Five
Vlad The Impaler
A Miracle Of Their Own (with Tim Rappleye)

Contents

'Keith Gave was this asshole who wrote a column for the Detroit Free Press. We never got along because he was always one of those reporters that was just waiting for something, so he could report the shit, you know?'

—Bob Probert, in his book, 'Tough Guy.'

For the fans

Foreword

Very much like when I came to Detroit two decades later, Montreal in the early 1970s was a team in transition when I first started coaching there. We won the Stanley Cup in my second year there, but really we were probably the third best team in the National Hockey League. We were far from a great team.

Sam Pollock, the general manager, had made some great draft choices—Guy Lafleur first overall in 1971, Steve Shutt fourth overall in 1972, and we got Bob Gainey with the No. 8 pick in 1973. They were young, but when they began to mature, all of a sudden we had a pretty good team. It wasn't until 1974, however, when we got two guys in the first round who wound up being great role players, that our team really started to transform.

We drafted Doug Risebrough with the seventh overall pick, and then five picks later we got Mario Tromblay. Neither was an elite offensive player, but both those guys were really smart players who could fight. They weren't heavyweights, more like middleweights. But nobody their size was going to beat them. They didn't have to fight the big guys because we had some big guys, too. And those guys didn't fight much anyway.

Suddenly, teams weren't pushing us around anymore. Then we brought up a guy we had in the minors, Yvon Lambert, who was actually drafted by Detroit. But just as he was coming into his own, Ned Harkness traded him to us. Now we had a pretty good line of players who knew their role and accepted it: scrappy, great defensively, almost impossible to score against but able to contribute offensively, too.

Those three guys, on a team with seven or eight Hall of Famers, made all the difference.

That's the thing that people don't realize about good role players. We might have had a star-studded lineup, but when we'd go into some places I wanted to set the table—establish a trend right from the outset as to how we intended to play that night. In Detroit, that's when I would always try to start Kris Draper, Kirk Maltby, and either Joe Kocur or Darren McCarty—for the simple fact that they were not going to be outworked.

They may not score, but neither would the other team. And their work ethic would spill over to the rest of the team. That's what made Steve Yzerman the player he was. He might have been a skilled player, but he was also a worker. He didn't take games off. Neither did those guys who played for me on the Grind Line, one of the most important units in all those years from the first Stanley Cup title in 1997 to the last of four in 2008.

By the time that line came together, Detroit had had some very good luck in the draft. In 1989, they got Hall of Famers Nicklas Lidstrom and Sergei Fedorov, along with Vladimir Konstantinov, who was on his way to the Hall of Fame before his career was ended in that limo crash. In 1990, the Wings added Slava Kozlov in the third round and used a second-round pick in 1992 to select Darren McCarty.

Finally, Detroit was adding some extraordinary talent in a nucleus of support around Yzerman. But, as some of those early

exits in the playoffs suggested, our roster was still a work in progress. It wasn't until we made a couple more trades that I felt we
finally had a team to make a serious run in the postseason. We got
Kris Draper in a 1993 trade with Winnipeg and, a few years later,
we got Kirk Maltby from Edmonton. What's interesting is at the
time, both trades were considered minor deals--made to bolster
the minor-league club in Adirondack, not necessarily to crack the
lineup in Detroit.

Maltby was surprised we traded for him. He looked at our
roster and wondered how he would ever get any ice time. But he's
the kind of player who enjoys making his presence known with his
play. Loved to hit, and he was a pretty good agitator who embraced
his role. So he fit right in.

But it was Draper who really helped to flesh out our roster, on
and off the ice. He always had a lot of energy, always a pepper pot,
always positive. I don't think I ever saw him get discouraged. He
was a really good skater, and he was excellent in the face-off circle.
Winning face-offs is all desire, and I think Kris felt he had to go out
and win face-offs or he'd never get on the ice.

The truth is we couldn't keep him out of the lineup. But it was
a challenge. At one point early on, I had to have a talk with Kris
and explain to him that we have Yzerman and Fedorov and Igor
Larionov at center. "I just didn't have enough time on the clock," I
told him. "You're going to be an important player on our team, but
not in the same way. You're going to be a role player." He accepted
it, and Draper and Maltby seemed to really enjoy playing together.
McCarty was a good fit on the right side, and when we brought Joe
Kocur back out of retirement, he fit well there, too. Both he and
McCarty were smart players who competed with a physical edge
that everyone in the NHL respected. I could play either of them
with Draper and Maltby, and whoever wasn't on that line I'd put
on Yzerman's wing to keep the flies off him.

But I have to say, and this is important, it's very difficult for players to accept being a role player for two reasons: No. 1, they don't get the ice time they need to produce offense; and No. 2, when you don't produce much offense, you don't get paid much either. It's not an easy job, because you're usually playing against the best players on the other team. Still, every one of those players managed to score some important goals for us, especially in the playoffs.

It takes a special type of player to do that. And on the Grind Line in Detroit, we had four of them.

Scott Bowman
February 2024

Ukes, Krauts and Coneheads

Clark Gilles rose from the bench at his stall, and the New York Islanders' dressing room immediately went silent.

"I remember, he was like John Wayne, or The Marlboro Man," teammate Bryan Trottier told a radio interviewer. Gilles, the National Hockey League's preeminent power forward on a team at the cusp of winning four straight Stanley Cup titles, was a man who believed that actions spoke louder than words. So when he spoke, people tended to listen. Carefully.

The subject of the moment was naming his line—a serious business in hockey circles. Nicknaming forward lines was once upon a time one of the more colorful traditions in the sport, one that has waned in recent years. For that, we can blame free agency's revolving door; players move from team to team with such frequency that three guys playing together long enough to establish an identity, and maybe earn a nickname, is fairly rare. (The Perfection Line in Boston was the recent exception that proved the rule as the calendar rolled into the 2020s.)

We can also blame the coaching carousel. With so much pressure to win in today's 32-team NHL, coaches are quick to mix things up, try different line combinations at the first sign of adversity. For most, it's a matter of acting swiftly or risk hitting the unemployment line. That carousel slows for no man.

Line naming—the topic Gilles was about to address—is an inexact art form. Nicknames often originate in the media. Some clever writer or broadcaster up in the press box will refer to a certain group with a colorful moniker it winds up in the sports pages or on the air, and it sticks. Sometimes, as in the case of the Islanders at that moment, a name will come from the team's public relations/ marketing staff. And soon, the team hopes, it will adorn pricey merchandize in the club's souvenir shop.

Other times, it'll come straight from the players, as Gilles would soon decree.

It didn't take long after coach Al Arbour put them together for the line of Gillies, Trottier and Mike Bossy to find success. Trottier, the playmaking center who played a sterling 200-foot game; Gillies, whose size and toughness made it impossible to move him from the front of the net; and Bossy, arguably the greatest pure goal scorer in the history of the game. They were electric together, and it didn't take long for one of the forward thinkers in the Isles' media department to suggest a public campaign to name the group.

At the time, as Trottier recalls in his book ("All Roads Home, A Life On And Off The Ice," McLelland and Stewart, 2022) and in interviews, there were some worthy line names around the league. Like the French Connection in Buffalo, the Triple Crown Line in Los Angeles, among others. So in a meeting with the players that included the media and members of the club's executive staff, the marketing man started to unveil the plan. Until then, the unit— which at times deployed other wingers before Bossy—had been known locally as the LILCO Line. That was the household acronym for the Long Island Lighting Company, the power conglomerate that provided the juice to light the red lamp behind the goaltenders, as the line did with spectacular regularity. A good name, to be sure, but it didn't get much play beyond the New York metropolitan area. This group deserved something better, according to prevailing wisdom.

"We need a good name for our Trottier-Gillies-Bossy line," the PR guy said, "so we're going to have a contest, open it up to everyone—fans, the media. . ."

That's when Gillies slowly rose, ending the marketing guy's message in mid-sentence.

"First of all, it's not the Trottier-Gillies-Bossy line," the big man said. "It's the Gillies-Trottier-Bossy line." And no one argued.

"He always wanted his name first. We didn't care," Trottier said as he recalled the moment.

Gillies continued: "And there ain't gonna be no contest. You can just call us The Trio Grande."

Discussion over. Dynasty at the starting gate.

"Clarkie, I love that. It's the best name ever!" Trottier told him later.

"Thank you," Clark responded. And so it was.

"What made our line so successful was a friendship, a chemistry, a bond all three of us shared," Trottier told a CBC interviewer.

The Trio Grande (GRAN-day, say it right like Gilles declared) led the Islanders to four straight Stanley Cup titles in the early 1980s. All three were inducted into the Hockey Hall of Fame. And if there were a hall of fame for line nicknames, The Trio Grande would be there as well.

Here, in no particular order, are a few others that should be considered, as well:

The Production Line
Detroit Red Wings – Ted Lindsay, Sid Abel and Gordie Howe, one of the most iconic lines in the history of the sport. Rarely has a unit like this identified more with a city, producing points and

Stanley Cup titles with the same, workmanlike consistency as the city's blue-collar workers on the automotive production plants. The line finished 1-2-3 in scoring in 1949-50. Lindsay led the way with seventy-eight points; Abel contributed sixty-nine and Howe sixty-eight . The Wings went on to defeat Toronto for the Stanley Cup that spring and continued to produce.

It also had two later iterations:

Production Line II, with Alex Delvecchio succeeding the retired Abel in a seamless transition.

Production Line III, with Frank Mahovlich replacing Lindsay at left wing after General Manager Jack Adams sent Lindsay packing with an ill-advised trade to Chicago.

The French Connection
Buffalo Sabres – Rick Martin, Rene Robert and Gilbert Perreault. Named after the popular movie at the time, the trio was a fixture at The Aud from 1972-79, dazzling audiences and leading the Sabres to the Stanley Cup Final in 1975.

The Triple Crown Line
Los Angeles Kings – Dave Taylor, Marcel Dionne and Charlie Simmer. A line fit for Kings, regal in every way, and one of the league's most prolific scoring units. In 1979-80 the group produced 146 goals, 328 points and played as a unit in the NHL All-Star Game at the Montreal Forum.

The Legion of Doom
Philadelphia Flyers – John LeClair, Mikael Renberg and Eric Lindros. If ever a unit commanded to be named, it was this one. Several nicknames were tossed around when the unit was formed in 1995: Bob's Big Boys (referring to GM Bobby Clarke), The

Doom, Gloom and Zoom Line, the JEM Line (initials of their first names) and The Crazy Apes. And why not? LeClair stood 6-foot-3 and weighed 226 points. Lindros went 6-4, 240, and Renberg 6-2, 235. They looked and sometimes acted the part of modern-day Broad Street Bullies. Which prompted Flyers teammate Jim Montgomery to suggest that the three "look like the Legion of Doom out there." The name stuck. For the record, their last appearance together was against Detroit. One of the most physically dominant and feared lines of all-time—at least until they faced the Red Wings in the 1997 Stanley Cup Finals, when they pretty much went AWOL. They were never seen together again.

The GAG Line

New York Rangers – Vick Hadfield, Jean Ratelle and Rod Gilbert. Lines tagged with letters are generally uninspiring. Most often, they represent initials of the three players' first or last names, creating a kind of shorthand for sports writers and fans. Not this one. And the joke (gag) was on the opponents, as the brightest line on Broadway in the early 1970s produced at a rate of more than a goal a game. Goal a game. Get it?

The Kraut Line

Boston Bruins – Bobby Bauer, Woody Dumart and Milt Schmidt. The NHL was never shy about celebrating its diversity, even as an upstart league barely a decade old when the Bruins formed this trio, all proud of their German heritage. After growing up together in Kitchener, Ontario, a German enclave that boasts the world's largest Oktoberfest outside of Germany. The three played together from the late 1930s to the mid-1940s—and Bruins fans cheered them all through World War II.

The Uke Line
Boston Bruins – Johnny Buyck, Bronco Horvath and Vick Stasiuk. Another dominant Bruins line from 1957-61, all very proud of their Ukrainian ancestry.

The Punch Line
Montreal Canadiens – Maurice Richard, Elmer Lach and Toe Blake. Named for its offensive explosiveness, and rightly so. The line dominated for four years in the 1940s, helping to win the Stanley Cup twice. In the 1944-45 season, the trio finished 1-2-3 in league scoring, Lach with eighty points, Richard with seventy-three and Blake with sixty-seven.

The Century Line
Pittsburgh Penguins – Before Sid and Gene, even before Mario and Jaromir, there was Syl Apps Jr., Lowell MacDonald and Jean Pronovost, who helped put a beleaguered expansion club on the NHL map. They had an uncommon ability to produce points for a team that was overmatched most nights. They combined for more than 100 goals and 200 points in four straight seasons in the 1970s, leading the Penguins to their first two seasons finishing above .500 in the standings.

The Coneheads
United States of America Men's National Team – 1980 Olympians Mark Pavelich, John Harrington and Buzz Schneider. Finding chemistry on a roster divided by geography—East Coast hockey elitists vs. the pride of the Midwest, predominately in Minnesota and Wisconsin—coach Herb Brooks experimented by putting together three guys who grew up playing shinny on ponds in the Iron Range of Northeast Minnesota. They clicked immediately and adopted

their name, The Coneheads, after an enormously popular skit on a relatively new sketch comedy show that was taking the nation by storm. When Team USA assistant coach Craig Patrick explained the line's name to Brooks, he shrugged. The Miracle on Ice coach had never heard of The Coneheads. Or the TV show, *Saturday Night Live*.

The Dynasty Line

Montreal Canadiens – Steve Shutt, Guy Lafleur and Jacques Lemaire. Dynasty might be an understatement in this era with a team coached to greatness by Scotty Bowman. The line was a cornerstone unit through the 1970s. But as good as they were together, they were not joined at the hip like some iconic lines. Bowman, as he tended to do, tweaked the unit from time to time, deploying Frank Mahovlich at center in place of Lemaire. That prompted the ever-clever Shutt to call it The Donut Line because, he said, "it has no firm center."

The Mafia Line

New York Rangers – Phil Esposito, Don Maloney and Don Murdoch. Whoever suggested there were five organized crime families in New York City may have erred. Some clever sports writer in town suggested there were six the way Espo—"The Godfather"—and his two "Dons" terrorized opponents in the late 1970s. May well be the cleverest of all these nicknames.

The Perfection Line

Boston Bruins – Patrice Bergeron, Brad Marchand and David Pastrnak. A nickname Boston fans loathe, which may be prone to hyperbole. Or maybe not. Arguably the most dominant line in the NHL over the last twenty-five years with its combination of defense and 200-foot playmaking (Bergeron), one of the best snipers of his era

(Pastrnak) and wretched peskiness combined with all-around skill in a guy (Marchand) who will do anything to win, including some cheap-shot stickwork and a propensity to even tongue-slobber an opponent to get him off his game. A unit with uncanny chemistry for the better part of seven seasons until Bergeron—one of the best defensive forwards to ever play the game—retired in 2023.

The KLM Line

Soviet Red Army Club (CSKA) – Vladimir Krutov, Igor Larionov and Sergei Makarov. Obviously one of those sportswriter short-hand line names, borrowing the last-name initial of each of the forwards. But the Soviets didn't run in three-man forward lines like it's done in North America. They deploy five-man units. Krutov, Larionov and Makarov played exclusively with the defensive pair, Slava Fetisov and Alexei Kasatonov. Together, the five were known as The Green Line, named simply for the color of their practice sweaters. Detroit's handful of former Soviet players, which included Larionov and Fetisov, were stamped as The Russian Five. The three forwards, Larionov flanked by Sergei Fedorov and Slava Kozlov, didn't have—and never wanted—a separate line name.

The Black Aces

Buffalo Ankerites – Herb Carnegie, Ossie Carnegie and Manny McIntire, the first all-black line in the semiprofessional Quebec Provincial League, which competed in mining towns in northern Ontario and Quebec in the 1940s. The group was recognized as much for their talent and skill as for their skin color. Herb Carnegie, a center, is widely known as the first great black hockey star, named league MVP in 1946, 1947 and 1948. He was given a tryout by the New York Rangers in 1948 and offered a contract to play in the Rangers' minor-league system. But he was offered less money than he was earning in the Quebec league, so he turned down all three offers the Rangers made.

E=MC²

New York Islanders – Matt Martin, Cal Clutterbuck and Casey Cizikas. One of the more creative and cerebral line names. This was a group opponents never wanted to play against with its combination of size, speed, toughness and a habit of scoring timely goals. The unit combined for 829 hits during the 2014-15 season. Pure energy (E) produced by Martin (M) and Clutterbuck and Cizikas (C2). Credit former Islander-turned-broadcaster Butch Goring for the unique moniker. Credit iconic Hockey Night In Canada analyst Don Cherry for his trademark hyperbole when he called it the best fourth line of all time. Open to debate, obviously. Starting with this book.

Two Kids and An Old Goat

Detroit Red Wings – Brett Hull, Pavel Datsyuk, Boyd Devereaux and Henrik Zetterberg. This one arguably should not qualify for this list, though Wings fans of a certain age will remember it fondly. Detroit was a team in transition in 2001-02, a "maturing" roster complemented by a pair of future Hockey Hall of Famers. Coach Scotty Bowman deployed one of those stars, Hull, then thirty-seven, with a couple of youngsters, Datsyuk and Devereaux, both twenty-three. En route to their third Stanley Cup title in six seasons, the self-deprecating Hull named the line. A year later, Hull found himself with Datsyuk and Zetterberg, the stars of the next generation who learned at the knee of one of the game's greatest goal-scorers, Both were destined to join Hull in the Hockey Hall of Fame. Their job, at that point in their careers, was to get Hull the puck, and they did it masterfully.

The Crash Line

New Jersey Devils – Former Red Wing Randy McKay, Bobby Holik and Mike Peluso. United by coach Jacques Lemaire to counter the larger skilled players in the Eastern Conference, players like Eric Lindros, Jaromir Jagr and Cam Neely. The Crash Line mates averaged 215 pounds and played an aggressive, physical style with no small amount of offensive upside. And crash they did. Just ask the Red Wings. Detroit was heavily favored to end a forty--year Stanley Cup drought when they faced the Devils in the Stanley Cup Final in 1995. Many were predicting a sweep. It was. But the Wings were on the wrong end of it. As it turned out, the Crash Line had a lot to do with that. Afterward, some in the New York media were anointing the trio as the most famous and celebrated fourth line in NHL history. And perhaps they were, for a short time, until. . .

The Grind Line

Detroit Red Wings – Kirk Maltby, Kris Draper, Joe Kocur or Darren McCarty. Energetic, hard-hitting, agitating, mouthy, defense-minded, penalty-killing cornerstones on teams that won the Stanley Cup four times over an eleven-year span.

This is their story.

It's All in the Name

Given their widely divergent responsibilities for their teams, it is practically impossible to reasonably compare the two most iconic forward lines in Detroit Red Wings history–The Production Line and The Grind Line.

Or is it?

To be sure, Gordie Howe and Ted Lindsay, flanking Sid Abel, was the engine that ran those teams in the late 1940s into the dynastic 1950s. They piled up the points and racked up scoring titles, trophies, Stanley Cups and championship rings. And The Grind Line? A bunch of plumbers and pipefitters, eh? They embraced the uglier side of hockey, doing their team's dirty work, providing much-needed energy, no small amount of thundering body checks, a dose of threatening intimidation and more than their share of timely offense. And they did it with unbridled enthusiasm and panache that made them fan favorites for more than a decade of unbridled success.

So yes, you're damned right we're going to compare the two most famous Red Wings lines—the way serious comparisons are made in hockey. The only way, really. Consider this:

Gordie Howe and Ted Lindsay, the two mainstays on The

Production Line, won the Stanley Cup four times each. Kris Draper and Kirk Maltby, the two inseparables on The Grind Line, won the Stanley Cup four times each. Abel won it three times, same as his successor, Alex Delvecchio. Darren McCarty like Draper and Maltby, owns four championship rings. The man McCarty rotated with, Joe Kocur, won it twice after an encore with the Wings.

Bottom line, the four men most associated with The Production Line, arguably the most famous line in National Hockey League history, have a combined fourteen Stanley Cup Rings. And the four members of The Grind Line? Yeah, fourteen. (Actually fifteen if you count the one Kocur earned with the Rangers in New York in 1994. He also won a ring as an assistant Wings coach in 2002.)

The point? The Grind Line is one of the most successful units in hockey history, and without peer among so-called fourth lines for those who insist on numbering them. It deserves its rightful place in Detroit shoulder to shoulder with The Production Line, those four men whose numbers hang from the rafters at Little Caesars Arena.

On April 20, 1997, John Wharton, the Red Wings' athletic therapist, was in the cramped trainer's area in the visiting dressing-room area at what was then known as the Kiel Center in downtown St. Louis. It was an off day—a maintenance day as players describe optional workouts when coaches are trying to conserve energy for when it's needed most. The Wings were between games three and four of the opening round of the 1997 Stanley Cup playoffs. Draper and Kocur were hanging out in the quiet area, a good place for Kocur to work on his crossword puzzles. Then the telephone rang. At the other end of the line was the club's merchandizing guru Mark Kirby with a rather pressing issue, at least to him.

"Hey John," Kirby said, "this line with Kris Draper, Joey Kocur and Kirk Maltby, they seem to have something going, eh? What do you think? Can we give them a name?"

"Your timing is perfect," Wharton responded. "A couple of them are right here. I'll put you on speaker phone."

Trainers' rooms have different vibes from team to team around the NHL. For some clubs, it's an off-limits area for players unless they need specific medical attention. Wharton had an open-door policy, and players would often stop by just to relax, have a cup of coffee and shoot the breeze. On this day, while Kocur was solving his puzzle, Maltby was relaxing with a cup of coffee, and Draper was getting in a little leg work. Speed was his calling card, and he took great care keep those wheels as strong, loose and healthy as possible.

So as Wharton hit the speaker button on the phone, he explained who was at the other end and why he was calling.

"You guys really do need a name," Wharton said.

And then it seemed like everybody started talking at once. Everyone but Kocur, engrossed in his puzzle.

Wharton remembers someone suggesting "The Bruise Cousins"—a spinoff from the "The Bruise Brothers," the tandem of Kocur with Bob Probert that terrorized opponents for several seasons from the mid-1980s to the early 1990s.

"How about the KDM line?" someone else suggested, using the last-name initials of each of the three Detroit players. Wharton immediately thought was too close to the famed Soviet Red Army forward line of Krutov, Larionov and Makarov (the KLM Line). In fact, Wharton suggested, it was so close it was bordering on being disrespectful.

During a lull in the conversation, with Kirby still listening in from Detroit, Wharton and Draper both seemed fixated on a certain word that has forever been in the common lexicon of nearly all hockey players.

"Let's keep in mind who you guys are. What you do for this team. You're a bunch of grinders; you're out there constantly grinding it out, wearing down opponents night after night—grinding them down. You're 'The Grind Line.'"

At that moment, Kocur looked up from his crossword. Turns out, he'd been multi-tasking, listening in on the conversation while he worked the puzzle. Now it was his turn to weigh in.

"That's it," he said. "We're 'The Grind Line.' I love it."

Kocur's career may have been resurrected just a few months earlier when he was signed out of a beer league, but his voice still carried immense gravitas in the room. Draper liked it, too, as did Maltby.

"So we're 'The Grind Line,'" Draper said.

"Sounds good to me," Kirby said, just before hanging up. "We're on it."

Within a few days, after some quick and creative design work, the Wings had hundreds of Grind Line T-shirts coming off the, uh, production line. And soon, there were thousands, adding exponentially to the merchandizing coffers of Mike and Marian Illitch's hockey club.

The next night, with their series tied with the St. Louis Blues at a game apiece, The Grind Line scored the opening goal—Draper, from Kocur and Maltby—in the first period. Detroit went on to win the game, 3-2, en route to a series victory in six games.

They were just getting started. But now they had a name.

The Mayor of Hockeytown

He came into the National Hockey League with a massive chip on his broad shoulder. And who could blame him?

There he sat in the stands at the Montreal Forum, surrounded by his family, listening to name after name being called at the podium, where NHL teams giddily laid claim to their newest, shiniest prospects. Forty-five of the so-called best and brightest teenaged prospects were selected in the league's entry draft that June 20, 1992, before the Detroit Red Wings took dibs on a confident, hard-nosed, high-scoring 6-foot-1, 209-pound right wing from the Belleville Bulls.

Darren McCarty was the forty-sixth of 264 players drafted that day, but considering some of the players taken ahead of him— including Detroit's first-round selection—it's easy to understand why he was still more than a little peeved by the time Red Wings public relations director Bill Jamieson finally introduced him to the small media contingent from Detroit.

General Manager Bryan Murray was overseeing the draft for the second time as Detroit's GM, and considering the team's haul the year before, he was fairly immune from the second-guessing that would come later. Most general managers will acknowledge that a successful draft is getting two players who can make an NHL roster for even a handful of seasons. In 1991, Murray's scouting staff led by Ken Holland went four-for-four at the top of the draft: winger Martin Lapointe, tenth overall; defenseman Jamie Pushor in the second round (thirty-second overall); goaltender Chris Osgood fifty-fourth overall; and winger Mike Knuble with their fourth pick (seventy-sixth overall). All four would be with the club at the start of its dynasty a few years later.

So it was with no small amount of confidence that the Wings selected Ottawa 67s left wing Curtis Bowen with Detroit's first-round pick, twenty-second overall.

Curtis Bowen? Are you kidding me? McCarty thought. After all, he'd played against Bowen in the Ontario Hockey League. Bowen was a year younger, but over a full season McCarty dominated in virtually every statistical category. Both played sixty-five games in their draft years. Bowen finished with thirty-one goals, forty-five assists for seventy-six points and ninety-four penalty minutes. McCarty, in his final junior season, had fifty-five goals among 127 points, winning the Jim Mahon Memorial Trophy as the league's top-scoring right wing. He also had 177 penalty minutes, a number indicative of the kind of player the Wings treasured.

Curtis Bowen. Who's that? Thirty-two years after that draft, I asked McCarty that question. We were sitting in a cigar bar in Birmingham, Michigan, puffing on cigars that cost more than a Ruth's Chris steak. He had that Dennis Rodman thing going with his hair; every time I ran into him it was a different style and color. At the moment, it was a misshapen Mohawk, tinged with fading red. And just as I finished the question, his eyes went ablaze with an incendiary glare that could have fired up a stogie two tables away.

"Who's Curtis Bowen?" McCarty snapped, a biting edge in his voice. "He was almost the answer to the greatest fuckup that the Detroit Red Wings ever made."

The one thing I've learned over the years—and we go back to that very day when his draft misery turned to joy—is to never ask a question for which you're not fully prepared for the way he might answer it. One of the most colorfully vocal players of his era, McCarty is rarely at a loss for words. "I never end my sentences with a period. It's dot. . . dot. . . dot. . . I always have something more to say."

Especially regarding the subject of that draft day. And if you're offended by certain language that some folks in polite society might find offensive, then tread lightly. Perhaps avoid the passages within quotation marks for a few pages.

"I thought I would be their first-round pick," McCarty said of the Wings. "And when I didn't go, when they took Bowen, I thought, 'Oh fuck.' I mean, I know I crushed my interview with Detroit."

In a telephone interview from his Vernon, British Columbia home in early fall 2024, Holland said he remembered meeting with McCarty among several early round prospects just before the draft.

"What would you do if you were drafted by the Detroit Red Wings?" Holland asked McCarty.

The player responded with what might be considered a typical answer from a nervous kid trying to make a good impression. But Darren McCarty was not nervous, and he felt that telling the truth was the best way to make the best first impression. So he spoke like he meant it.

"Anything," he said. "I'll do anything." And then he rather boldly turned the question around. "What do you want me to do?" he asked. "Just tell me. I'll do it."

McCarty's response carried a certainty that made an impression. Yet Holland remained skeptical, even though Detroit's OHL scout Paul Crowley insisted that the prospect was worthy of a top pick. But there was a glaring flaw in McCarty's game, so Holland asked him about it, point blank.

"What about your skating," Holland asked. That's when McCarty dropped the metaphorical gloves.

"Mr. Holland, I am going to play in the National Hockey League," he said. "And nothing is going to stop me from playing in the National Hockey League."

Talk about making a strong first impression.

"He said it with enough conviction that I just believed him," Holland said. "It was just a gut instinct at the time, but it felt like he was sincere and determined to find some way to have an impact on an NHL team."

Holland may not have known it at the time, though he might have had an inkling, but he had just met a young man who needed a wheelbarrow to cart his balls around.

So with Bowen in the fold and teams picking off players early in the second round, McCarty was still sitting there with his family as the Wings' next selection approached. "And I'm just thinking, 'If you motherfuckers don't draft me here, I will come back and I will fucking haunt you.'"

Holland finally called McCarty's name, figuring that if he wasn't quite good enough to make it as a contributing bottom-six winger, then McCarty was tough enough to hang on as a role player willing to take on all comers as an efficient NHL middleweight enforcer. After hugging his parents (and a large contingent of family and friends) and taking the stage for the requisite Draft Day photos, McCarty was led to the Wings' table for handshakes all around. Then he was introduced to the few reporters from Detroit, and it was clear to me that he was thrilled to be drafted by his hometown team. Growing up just across the Detroit River in Southern Ontario, he was a devoted Wings fan. But he also admired the Edmonton Oilers. "I always thought that as a fan you really needed to have two teams, because one of them would probably suck." Which was a pretty good description of the Red Wings as McCarty was growing up. The Oilers, conversely, enjoyed a run of five Stanley Cup titles in a seven-year span that covered his formative years in hockey.

Two memories remain vivid from that conversation of ten minutes or so in Quebec. First, how much McCarty sounded like a sincere and proud Chamber of Commerce spokesman when we asked where he was from: "Leamington, Ontario, tomato capital of Canada!" he said. And later, during a one-on-one conversation, he shared how much he wanted those of us in the media to understand, to appreciate and to spread the word that the Detroit Red Wings had drafted a bona fide hockey player that day. And he promised to prove it.

"I'll tell you this," he said, looking me straight in the eye, "I might have been drafted in the second round, but I can play in this league. Count on it. You'll see."

As most teams do following that annual event, the Red Wings left the draft table at the Montreal Forum that summer feeling good about their haul, confident that at the very least they had acquired a couple of top-six wingers who stood a chance to become part of their core for years.

"I'll tell you what, our excitement over Curtis Bowen was unbelievable," said Doug MacLean, then Murray's associate coach who would eventually ascend to assistant general manager. "This was a kid who was every bit as hard-nosed as McCarty was in juniors. He was tough. He could score goals and he played a tough game, but he wasn't a fighter."

At training camp that fall, the reviews on Bowen were less than sterling. "He can't play," one of the team's star players told me after several days of camp. "All he does is chase the puck around the ice like a little kid. He's got no clue."

And the toughness wasn't evident either. For a first-round pick,

Bowen was virtually invisible even in intra-squad scrimmages. "I think he was afraid," an opposing NHL executive said. "He tried to play a tough game in juniors, but he couldn't back it up when it came to fighting. He would never fight."

As it turned out, Bowen played two more years of junior hockey with the 67s, then three undistinguished seasons with Adirondack of the American Hockey League before the Wings cut him loose. His career ended quietly across the pond with five seasons of low-level professional hockey in Great Britain. He never played a game in the NHL.

And McCarty? He just continued doing what he had done since he first laced up a pair of skates: proving people wrong by living up to his draft-day bravado.

Only Darren (he wasn't a McCarty yet) could turn a blessed occasion like his own birth into some kind of April Fools' prank-gone-wrong. Roberta Pritchard and Doug Francottie were high-school sweethearts, but their brief union ended quickly after their son was born on April 1, 1972. While Francottie pursued a career in law enforcement in British Columbia, Darren's mom bought a mobile home and parked it on property owned by her parents, Jean and Bob Pritchard, in rural South Woodslee, population about 200, just south of Lake St. Clair in Essex County, Ontario.

Shortly before he turned five, Darren's life changed dramatically when a man showed up to fix the air-conditioning unit on the mobile home. His name was Craig McCarty, and he would eventually become Darren's stepfather and a major influence in his life—despite a sometimes tumultuous relationship.

Darren took his first choppy strides on skates on the small rink Grandpa Pritchard built in his backyard when winters were cold enough to freeze over a sprinkled lawn. There was a creek in the back, too, that provided another skating surface. But for years, hockey was just another game to play among a multitude of sporting pursuits, especially baseball.

"Oh man, baseball was my first love," he said. "If I had my way, I'd have two Stanley Cups and two World Series rings."

He was twelve when the hometown Detroit Tigers won the 1984 World Series. By that age, McCarty was an elite-level catcher in his age group. So naturally, he says, "Lance Parrish was my guy."

Until about that age, McCarty could still dream of one day making it as far as Detroit's All-Star catcher. "I could hit a 100-mile-per-hour fastball when I was twelve years old," he said, adding that by that age his team had won three All-Ontario championships. His youth organization was not sanctioned by Little League Baseball, but if it had been, he believes, it could have represented Canada at the Little League World Series in Williamsport, Pennsylvania. But his baseball dreams ended shortly thereafter, when pitchers he was facing learned how to spin the baseball.

"When they started throwing that hook shit, I was done," he said. "I was better at punching people in the face."

By then he was warming up to his second favorite sport, which he didn't necessarily embrace at first. "My first year in hockey, I didn't get to play because I wouldn't wear the garter belt," he said. "I didn't like how it felt on my legs. So my parents said that if I won't wear the equipment, I can't play." A year later, he relented and volunteered to play goaltender.

"I was six, and I started out in net because I couldn't skate very well," he said. "I was so bad I learned how to stop by bodychecking. It was easier and more fun to just hit guys than it was to try and stop."

By then, the McCarty's family had moved to Leamington, where

Craig ran his HVAC business. Darren loved his new community—a big city, by comparison to Woodslee. Leamington, with a diverse population approaching thirty thousand when he was growing up there, is the second largest urban center in Essex County after Windsor. It includes Point Pelee National Park, the southernmost point of mainland Canada, on Lake Erie. "The greatest thing about it is that I didn't learn race," he said. "It didn't matter what race, color, religion or nationality. None of it mattered. As kids, we all just played."

Leamington also boasts some of the most fertile farmland on earth, hence, the tomato industry that has dominated the local economy for more than a century. The H.J. Heinz company set up shop in Leamington in 1908, making ketchup and other food products. Heinz operated the plant until 2014, when it was sold to Highbury Canco, which still produces tomato juice and other products for Heinz.

The region also holds the distinction for having the largest concentration of commercial greenhouses in all of North America, with nearly two thousand acres of greenhouse products, including tomatoes, peppers, cucumbers, roses and other flowers, and cannabis.

Like many youngsters in the region, Darren McCarty spent time in the tomato fields to try and make a quick buck. In his book, *My Last Fight, The True Story Of A Hockey Rock Star* (Triumph Books, 2013), McCarty tells of hitting the fields with his pal, Matt Derksen, a hard-throwing pitcher who broke McCarty's catching-hand thumb three times. Derksen's family owned the farm, and Derksen's father paid pickers fifty cents a bushel. At the end of a long, back-breaking day, the local Mennonite workers might have three hundred bushels, McCarty said in his book. "And we would have fifty. The problem was that we often used those tomatoes to perfect our throwing motion."

As good as he was at baseball, though, McCarty by now was head-over-heels in love with hockey. So much so that he was able to convince his stepfather to drop him off every morning at 6 a.m. so he could spend an hour skating and working on his shot; he had shunned the goaltender's pads to skate out.

"I liked scoring. And hitting," he said. "I was always the worst skater but the hardest worker." Hence the willingness to rise early and put in the extra time. For about a decade, until he was sixteen, he attended the Can-Am hockey school each summer at the University of Guelph, working and working and working on his game. His parents would pay the $400 fee for one week of camp. McCarty worked for his stepdad to earn $400 for an additional week. "I was digging holes and running ducts since I was ten years old," he said. "And I hated every minute of it.

"Craig McCarty was the father I wanted to make proud. He taught me about work ethic. He gave me the job I couldn't quit or get fired from. I always told him, 'If you die and leave me that business I'll sell it the next day.' That was my motivation to become a hockey player. In my life, I have to know what I don't want. I may not know what I want, but I know what I don't want."

By age fifteen, McCarty had an inkling of what he might want after scoring about eighty goals—by his count—in a season for the Leamington Raiders, a Major Bantam team. He had reached a crossroads in his hockey career, requiring a life-defining decision that would test his tight-knit family's resolve. Brian Drumm, the new coach of the Junior B Peterborough Roadrunners, was taking over a team that hadn't won a single game the season before. He recruited McCarty as a cornerstone winger with the promise that he could help him reach his full potential in hockey. The move from Bantam to Junior B hockey was not inconsequential. The players were older, the hockey a lot rougher. More concerning for Darren's parents: Peterborough was nearly three hundred miles away, nearly six hours by car away on the other side of Toronto.

While it is not unusual for the most promising young hockey players in Canada to leave home to compete at higher levels—it's common as well in the United States, Russia, Sweden, Finland, and other hockey-playing countries—it also is not an easy decision for many parents. When they list the pros and cons of such a move, the cons often outweigh the perceived positives. But the bottom line, for the McCartys and many others, was that they didn't want to stand in the way of their son chasing his dream, however much of a long shot it was for him to make it all the way to the NHL.

"My stepfather always said that you should never put yourself in a position to say, 'What if. . .'" McCarty wrote. "That's why I've always been balls-out in everything I've tried."

His parents were all in as well, showing their support by buying a cottage twenty minutes outside Peterborough so they could visit nearly every weekend. It was a challenge to the family budget, to be sure. But it speaks volumes for the kind of commitment some hockey families make. And besides, they weren't done raising that kid yet. Meantime, Drumm was true to his word, which is why McCarty will always count him among the most influential people in his life.

"He was my coach and my billet when I went to Peterborough," McCarty said, "and he gave me the secret. Once you tell me the secret, that's all I need. This is what he told me: 'If you want to get to the NHL, you've got to do one thing better than 99.99 percent of everybody else playing.'"

And for McCarty, Drumm said, that was physical play. To elaborate: the first year in every league, whether it's in a game, in practice, whatever, establish your physical game. Create some room for yourself. Once you have that room, work on your game. Develop your skills. Don't worry about stats. It's all about setting a tone for yourself.

This was music to McCarty's ears. For most of his young life, he had been told that "the one thing" that would keep him out of the NHL was his skating. He had a rather clunky stride, often described like he was running on skates. But now McCarty was hearing that "the one thing" that might get him to the NHL was physical, punishing hockey. And he was really good at beating guys up.

"I was fighting eighteen-year-olds when I was twelve," he said. "And holding my own." That was during his first NHL experience in the Nazzerine Hockey League. Every Sunday when the service ended at St. Michael's church, the boys would take to the ice and form groups by nationality—the Italians, the Portuguese, the Irish. "It would be like the IHL (International Hockey League," he said, referring to a kind of hockey with plenty of extracurricular fisticuffs. "I was one of the youngest guys, but that's how you learn."

"The fear, that never bothered me. I was battle-tested. Way better battle-tested off the ice than I was on the ice."

So he was grateful for Drumm's advice, and he took it to heart with no small amount of confidence. Another thing about Darren McCarty: he never needed to be told anything twice. "Dude, on the back of my hockey card all it needs to say is, 'Highly coachable.'"

He wasted little time in establishing this new version of himself. In a training camp scrimmage, he dropped the gloves and beat the hell out of one of the team's toughest players. The only problem was that his mother was watching from the stands

"I was not impressed," Roberta McCarty said in an October 2024 telephone interview from her home in South Woodslee. Which might have been an understatement. Darren remembers his mother being horrified to the point she wouldn't even talk to him. This was *not* what she had expected when she sent her son off to chase his dreams. Just following my coach's advice, trying to establish myself as a tough guy, Mom, he tried to explain.

Fast forward about 8½ years to March 26, 1997. Yes, Roberta

was at Joe Louis Arena for the infamous "paybacks are a bitch" game with the Colorado Avalanche. And no, she was not among the 20,000 or so fans on their feet cheering rabidly as her son rag-dolled and bloodied Claude Lemieux, finally getting revenge for Lemieux's unspeakable transgression the previous spring.

"It was all right across the ice from where we were sitting," she said. "I remember seeing some friends of ours before the game and telling them, 'Oh, I just hope it's a nice quiet game without too much hoopla.' Well, that didn't happen."

Most impressive, Roberta McCarty said, was that the Wings found a way to overcome a two-goal deficit late in the game and win in overtime.

By then, of course, she had come to accept her son's frequent fisticuffs, understanding that it was an important part of his resume in the NHL. Mother may not have endorsed her son's sudden transformation to tough guy in his first year in Peterborough, but Drumm's advice—create some room for yourself—turned out to be gold. McCarty played that Junior B season well enough to get noticed and be drafted by the Belleville Bulls, where he deployed the same strategy, creating a wide berth for himself and his teammates throughout the Ontario Hockey League.

"I only lost one fight in juniors, and in my last year I fought the guy again and beat the shit out of him," McCarty said, noting that his mother was there to see that, too. "By then, she had learned to understand it. That completed the evolution for her. That and my relationship with Brian Drumm—and her relationship with the understanding that this is what I needed to do to keep moving up."

By his third OHL season, in fact, McCarty was given so much room that it was almost laughable, especially on the Olympic-sized rink that Bellville called home. "If I came over the blue line and wound up, the D-man (defenseman) would back into the top of the crease because he didn't want to step up and get hit," he said.

Naturally, a lot of goals came on short-range slapshots. He finished the season at a nearly two-point-per-game clip over sixty-five games.

Thanks to the secret, and despite his skating deficiencies, McCarty was on to Detroit as a prized prospect. Dave Lewis, an assistant to coach Scotty Bowman, remembers bumping into McCarty shortly after he was drafted in that summer of 1992, when The Joe was set up for arena football.

"My son was in high school at the time, and he brought four or five buddies in to play football on the turf in the arena," said Lewis, whose wife was among the few spectators in the stands watching the boys play. Suddenly, she was approached by a polite young man.

"You think it would be all right if I played with these guys," the guy asked.

"Who are you?" Brenda Lewis asked.

"I'm Darren McCarty. I just got drafted by the Detroit Red Wings."

She said she felt pretty sure that would be OK, so he went down and played football with the boys for about an hour. "And that was his introduction to Joe Louis Arena," said Lewis, who remembers McCarty competing with the pigskin the same way he played hockey in those early days with the Wings.

"He was keen. He was eager. He was wide-eyed and raw," Lewis said. "As a hockey player, he had to get some refining done to his game, and when he did he turned out to be a heck of a player."

But it didn't come quickly or easily. Secret or not, professional hockey was an entirely new and demanding challenge.

"I'll never forget dealing with Darren when he first got to Detroit," said MacLean, who as general manager with Adirondack negotiated McCarty's first professional contract. McCarty got into a fight in an exhibition game. The Joe Louis Arena crowd, which adores its brawlers, was cheering wildly and McCarty was egging them on with his own antics as he was ushered to the penalty box.

"I was going bananas," McCarty recalled, "and I got scolded for that."

It was MacLean who did the scolding, telling the exuberant young winger that such behavior is not tolerated in Detroit. You drop the gloves, take care of business and skate to the penalty box. The JLA crowd doesn't need any more prompting.

Regarding the rest of his game, however, McCarty struggled mightily. "He got off to a really fricken tough start in Adirondack," MacLean. "Him and Marty Lapointe both were off to horrendous starts there. But Darren was a disaster."

Or not. MacLean may have been overreacting in his initial assessment of McCarty. As it turned out, McCarty was once again following Drumm's advice, though it was a lot harder in the professional ranks, and it took a little longer. Eventually, he had earned some room with his physical play. Now he could work on his skills, continue to develop. And he did, despite all the naysayers.

"I was always told that I couldn't skate well enough to play in the NHL. And my reponse was always, 'well, what do I have to do to get better?'" he said. "That's why every summer was about working out with (internationally renowned power-skating guru) Laura Stamm. Whatever I need to do, I put in the work. I even went to Sweden a couple of summers when I was already in the NHL. That's the way I am."

But before he could seriously work on his skating in his rookie pro season, he needed some room. And how did he manage that? "Forty-five fighting majors and 278 penalty minutes," he said. When he got a little room, the points started to come. He finished the season with a respectable seventeen goals among thirty-six points and a plus-sixteen rating in seventy-three games.

"Boy, did he ever come on," MacLean said. "He became a real player."

McCarty made the Detroit roster the following season, and he couldn't have imagined a more perfect time and place to begin his NHL career. "In Adirondack, fighting all those guys. I knew my role," he said. "The game was perfect back then, the physicality of it. It was easy. No matter how my day's going at work, I could go out, pick a fight, beat somebody up, and there on the scoreboard it says it all: I gave a shit."

As eager and willing as he was, McCarty's workload in Detroit, remarkably, got a little lighter. The reason? A guy named Bob Probert, the undisputed heavyweight champion in NHL history. (By then, Joe Kocur had been traded to the New York Rangers.)

"Probie could play, too, and team needed somebody like me to keep the fucking gnats off. If I'm fighting all the middle weights and light heavyweights to keep those guys off him, then I'm doing my job. That's team toughness. I knew once I got to Detroit that no one was ever going to take that role from me."

But the Probert-McCarty tag team lasted just a single season—Scotty Bowman's first behind the bench in Detroit after succeeding Murray. On July 15, 1994, Probert crashed his Harley in West Bloomfield Township, hitting a car, flying over the handlebars and landing, miraculously, on the only patch of grass surrounded by acres of concrete and asphalt. Authorities determined his blood alcohol level to be nearly triple the legal limit of .08 percent. There were also trace amounts of cocaine in his system, authorities reported. At the time of his accident, Probert was a free agent quite likely to re-sign with the Wings. Four days later, they cut him loose forever. "This is it. The end," senior vice-president Jimmy Devellano said, adding that in his twelve seasons in Detroit, to that point, the team had never spent more time or resources on one player and his problems than the Wings did on Probert.

Suddenly, McCarty was like the Lone Ranger in Detroit. Sure, they had a few other proven pugilists like wingers Brendan Shanahan and Martin Lapointe, but again players with their skills served the team better on the ice rather than in the penalty box. So McCarty enthusiastically took on all comers, even at his own peril.

"Oh man, Scotty saved my life—several times," McCarty said. "I remember one time against St. Louis, lining up for a face-off at the blue line in front of the bench, and Tony Twist is just egging me on. 'Come on, let's go. We're going now. We're going!' Now Tony Twist is like Joey Kocur. One punch and the guy can end your career.

"All of a sudden, Scotty puts his foot on the bench and leans over and yells, 'McCarty. McCarty! If you fight that fucking guy, you'll never play another shift for me again!'

"I just looked at Twist and said, 'You heard the man. Sorry.'"

The puck dropped. Play resumed. And McCarty breathed a massive sigh of relief.

———◆———

Scotty Bowman didn't coach forward lines. He preferred to find a pair, typically a center and a winger, who worked well together. The third player on that line would provide the ingredient the coach wanted on the ice at the time. Besides toughness, McCarty was a sound defensive player known to chip in the odd goal. He was also strong in the face-off circle, winning, by his estimation, nearly 60 percent of the draws he took in his career. For his first several years in Detroit, McCarty never knew from shift to shift who might be his linemates. But with his combination of skills, he never lacked for ice time.

"Sometimes I'd play with Stevie, sometimes with Sergei and sometimes with Iggy (Igor) Larionov," McCarty said. "We never knew. We all practiced or played with everybody else. We would practice with certain lines and wonder, 'What the fuck are these guys on the same line for?' Then we'd start the game with four different lines. Then we'd be sitting there during the game and Scotty would go, 'You, you and you, you're up next.' We called it 'bench bingo.' We'd look at each other, then we'd go out and score, come back and sit down. And somebody would say, 'Bingo!'

"More times than not, it happened. That's accountability. We all could play in different spots. That's how Scotty built us."

Bowman also built the best team—the best lockerroom—McCarty had ever experienced, creating a culture borne of the players' love-hate relationships with their coach. Scotty Bowman didn't always have the warmest bedside manner with some of his players; some despised him for that. But they all loved winning, and they did a lot of that with him behind the bench.

"He wasn't just a great coach but a great psychologist, too," McCarty said. "And he did it where it was always us against him. He made it so there were no cliques. Walk into the room and we all had this special relationship with each other—and that exists to this day whenever we see one another. Scotty just knew. . . he finds out what makes you tick, and he figures out how to get the best out of all of us."

There was no greater evidence of that tight-knit camaraderie than the night of March 26, 1997, when archrival Colorado visited Joe Louis Arena for the fourth and final meeting between the two teams. The Red Wings felt they had some unfinished business to tend to, a little retribution for the serious facial injuries Kris Draper sustained the previous spring when he was hit from behind by Claude Lemieux. Detroit's true heavyweight Joe Kocur, back in Detroit for the twilight of his career, was not in the lineup due to illness. Didn't matter. Since the moment McCarty drove Draper home after his mouth was wired shut to help repair a badly broken jaw, this was the night McCarty claimed for himself. He neither wanted, needed nor expected any help.

And Scotty Bowman knew it. So when he saw Lemieux take the ice on Peter Forsberg's wing late in the first period, Bowman sent out his two biggest, toughest wingers—McCarty and Brendan Shanahan, flanking center Igor Larionov, the smallest player on either team. Incredibly ironic, it was Larionov who lit the match. Tired of getting hit from behind with Forsberg's stick, Larionov finally turned, grabbed Forsberg in a headlock and threw the only two punches he ever threw in his Hall of Fame career as he wrestled his opponent to the ice.

That's when McCarty went looking for Lemieux, who declined the request for a dance. Instead, the gutless Avalanche forward retreated to a fetal position beneath his helmet. The rest, including McCarty's game-winning goal thirty-seven seconds into overtime, is history, celebrated each year in Detroit as "Turtle Day."

Now the Red Wings were ready for the playoffs, and Bowman seemed to feel as content with his myriad line combinations as he'd ever get. While the Russian Five was his nuclear option, the forwards in that group—Larionov flanked by Sergei Fedorov and Slava Kozlov—were often split up. Fedorov frequently centered Kozlov and Doug Brown(ov). Larionov was often between Shanahan and Martin Lapointe. Steve Yzerman typically centered late-season acquisition Tomas Sandstrom on the left wing and McCarty on the right. And his go-to line in critical defensive situations always involved center Kris Draper between Kirk Maltby and, most often, Joe Kocur. But Scotty being Scotty. . . The coach, as they say, had a lot of toys in the attic, and he liked to play with them all.

Kocur played a critical role after being signed out of an adult recreation league in suburban Detroit, an encore performance worthy of an Oscar for his calming influence on a team that faced so much pressure to win. He'd been to the mountaintop, his name engraved in silver on the Stanley Cup. "Just relax and play your game," he would tell his teammates. "We're made for this moment."

While Kocur was a fixture on the Grind Line, Bowman occasionally swapped him out for McCarty and Kocur would ride shotgun with Yzerman. It all depended on the situation. Which players to have on the ice and when? This was the genius that set Bowman apart from any other who coached the game. That's what made the start of 1997 Stanley Cup Final in Philadelphia so memorable. All those stars, those eventual Hall of Famers—Yzerman, Fedorov, Shanahan, Larionov—and Scotty Bowman has something else in mind.

"That first shift," McCarty said, his eyes lighting up again. "That's one of my favorite photos ever, of the opening face-off in Philly. It's me, Malts and Drapes. I'm adjusting my elbow pad. It's like, 'Lock and load, baby. Here we come.' That first shift I almost put (Flyers defenseman) Petr Svoboda in the eighth row, I hit him so hard."

The Grind Line scored the first two Detroit goals, both in the first period, of a 4-1 Wings' victory. Maltby scored shorthanded in the game's seventh minute on an assist from Draper, and Kocur, now on right wing with McCarty moved to Yzerman's wing, scored a gorgeous unassisted goal after intercepting a pass late in the period.

"We all could play in different spots. That was the beauty of Scotty's system," McCarty said. But there was something different, something at once indefinable and remarkable, about playing on the Grind Line. "It was like we were playing with one brain. The biggest thing is, we trusted each other. With Malts and Drapes, they trusted the fact that I wasn't going to let anything happen to them."

Both Maltby and Draper readily acknowledge that their non-stop yapping would occasionally get them in trouble. Their mouths would sometimes write checks that their asses couldn't cash. Which is where McCarty (and certainly Kocur) came in. It happened a lot.

"OK, what the hell is going on here," McCarty would yell, skating into a scrum.

"That Draper. That Maltby, what a bunch of fucking assholes," would often be the reply from an opponent who decided he'd taken just about enough from those guys.

"Yeah, I know they are," McCarty responded. "But they're my assholes. You keep your fucking hands off them."

And that would be that.

"I was the nice guy. I'd cut them a deal," McCarty said with a smirk. Message received.

"With their speed and their physicality, they were really hard to play against," McCarty said of his Grind Line mates. "Here's the thing: You didn't want to play against us because we were coming at you in waves. Other teams would try to get out of the matchup because we always played against their top lines, and they didn't want to play that way. We were relentless."

Relentless until the very end, when the guy they said couldn't skate did that improbable, sensational impression of Sergei Fedorov to ice Detroit's first Stanley Cup championship in forty-two years. The play started deep in the Detroit end, with defenseman Vladimir Konstantinov taking a hit (as usual) to make a play (as usual), chipping the puck to Yzerman, who backhanded it to Sandstrom. McCarty found an opening at the blue line, and Sandstrom hit him with a tape-to-tape pass.

Now McCarty was off alone with just one defenseman to beat. And he did, with arguably the greatest move in his hockey career. He deked Janne Niinimaa out of his pads, faked a forehand maneuver and cruised around the defenseman on the backhand side. Now he was all alone, with goaltender Ron Hextall about fifteen feet away, panic-stricken and already sprawled on the ice at the left corner of the crease. McCarty easily cut to his right past the goalie and tucked the puck into an yawning yet for a 2-0 Detroit lead with nearly twenty-seven minutes left to play in the game. That's when Detroit, led by the Grind Line, went into lockdown mode, helping to keep the Flyers off the scoreboard until just 15 seconds remained in the game. Lindros scored his lone goal of the series.

"That's why every year the first Christmas card goes to Eric Lindros," McCarty likes to say."Why? Because his goal made mine the Stanley Cup-winning goal."

The rest of the story is fairly well known, at least part of it: back-to-back Stanley Cups in 1997-98, and another in 2002, with the Grind Line playing a critical role. But it cannot be told without an important post-script. McCarty enjoyed his rock-star status around Detroit to a fault, and, admittedly, he eventually he lost his way.

"He lost his priorities," Holland said. After the third Stanley Cup title in six seasons, hockey became an afterthought for McCarty. "I remember sitting him down and talking to him about his priorities. I told him that when we get up to Traverse City for training camp, I didn't want to hear that his band was up there playing. Sure enough, we go to camp, and he's up there with his band. It pissed me off."

When the league shut down for the entire 2004-05 season because of a labor dispute, McCarty went balls out on his music career with his band, Grinder.

"My own fault," he said. "Hockey was no longer my No. 1 priority. The game had changed. It was just. . . different. And you have to understand, hockey is what I did. It's not who I am. There are so many other things."

But fronting a glorified garage band can be expensive, especially with a tricked-out touring bus to get from gig to gig. By the time the NHL resumed play in 2005, McCarty was broke and declaring bankruptcy. Worse, the Wings were cutting him loose. In what was then an easy decision for Holland, the club bought McCarty out of his contract. He was done in Detroit and entertaining all offers. Sort of.

"Colorado came at me hard," he said, noting that former Red Wing Brad (Motor City Smitty) Smith, the Avalanche's Windsor-born director of player personnel, did the recruiting. "There was no way I was going to Colorado. No way. It wasn't out of disrespect, but there are just certain non-negotiables."

McCarty ended up accepting less money to play in Calgary for Daryl Sutter, the former Chicago Blackhawk captain who went on to enjoy a long and successful career as a coach and general manager. "When he came calling, I was all in," McCarty said. And that first year out there was so much fun. We made the playoffs, got up 3-2 in the first round to Anaheim and lost in seven. That was tough, especially when Anaheim went on to win the Cup."

Things went from bad to worse quickly. "Unfortunately that summer I relapsed after ten years," he said, "and I went downhill real quick."

When the season began that fall of 2006, the Flames had a new coach behind the bench. Sutter had replaced himself with Jim Playfair, who didn't seem to value McCarty's potential to help the team nearly as much as Sutter did. "We didn't see eye to eye at all," McCarty said, rather diplomatically.

He had appeared in just thirty-two games for Calgary that season—without scoring a single point. His contract was up and his career appeared to be over. At least everyone seemed to believe that except for Darren McCarty. He refused accept that it was over for him despite battling through the darkest days of his life—another failed relationship, more money problems—all detailed in his brutally honest biography, *My Last Fight*. While he was working hard to clean up his life, he began to lobby his former linemate and best friend, Kris Draper.

"Drapes, I gotta know. *I've got to know!*" McCarty pleaded.

"Mac, I'll do whatever it takes, but you've got to be there. You've got to show up," Draper responded.

And he did, going to court to get his trainwreck of a personal life in order. Cleaning himself up. Getting himself in NHL condition again. But Holland remained more than a little skeptical.

"I ended up meeting with him a couple of times, giving him some guidance, trying to figure out a way he might be able to help our club," Holland said. "I thought he'd be fabulous on the radio. But he still wanted to play. So I thought about it and thought about it."

Eventually, the heart overruled his brain, Holland said.

"Listen, I have a soft spot for Darren McCarty. "It's hard not to, if you know him. He's blue collar. There was always something between him and the fans. He's Darren McCarty!"

Convinced that the player had gotten his life back in decent order, Holland talked it over with coach Mike Babcock. Ultimately, they decided to give McCarty a shot. His first step back was a tryout with the Flint Generals of the International Hockey League.

"And I loved it," he said. "It was like I went full circle, back to my rookie year in '93 with Adirondack. I got my love of the game back. Even got on the power play." He scored three goals and six points in 11 games in Flint before Holland signed him to a contract and sent him to Grand Rapids. McCarty scored a hat trick in his first game there and afterwards started thinking, *OK, we've got something cooking here.*

Meantime, McCarty kept lobbying, telling anyone who would listen that he belonged back in Detroit. "I know I have something left, but this isn't just about me," he told Draper. "Those are my guys in that locker room, and even though I wasn't there I knew that they needed me. They needed that buffer in the locker room because of Babcock."

Universally despised by his players in Detroit, Babcock eventually called McCarty to Detroit with three games left in the 2007-08 regular season. McCarty still gets chills thinking about it, and those chills were contagious across the table in that smoke-filled cigar bar.

"I don't care what anybody says about him, I'll always be grateful to Mike Babcock for it," he said. "That first game back, the opening face-off at St. Louis. I remember looking over at Malts, at Drapes. The Grind Line is back, baby! How cool was that?"

McCarty managed just one assist in those final three regular-season games, playing with a broken rib that he managed to keep fairly secret. That post-season, he scored a goal and an assist with nineteen penalty minutes, playing seventeen of twenty-two playoff games to help the Red Wings win their fourth Stanley Cup in a span of 11 seasons. Once again, defying enormous odds in the process.

"I just remember thinking, it's not even about winning the Cup or anything," he said. "To me, it was about how, in life, no matter what. . . I don't think I'm special, but I do think I have a bit of a superpower. And if I can hone in on that superpower, I can accomplish anything I put my mind to—just by doing what needs to be done."

That's the same attitude he had when he left hockey forever and pursue other endeavors, like starring in his own comedy troupe, managing pro wrestlers and starting his own cannabis line. Always the McCarty way: balls out. *Hockey is what I did; it's not who I am.*

Red Wings owners Marian and Mike Ilitch were notorious for

throwing immense celebrations at their home to commemorate certain events, and two memories are seared into McCarty's brain forever. The first was the biggest mountain of chilled jumbo shrimp he had ever seen. The second was a short conversation with coach Scotty Bowman, who had announced his retirement after the 2002 Stanley Cup win. In a heartfelt address to his team before Game Seven of the Western Conference final against archrival Colorado, Bowman acknowledged that one of the things he had recently come to realize is that he never told his players how much he appreciated them.

"So we're at this party, and Scotty walks up to me," McCarty recalled.

"Hey Mac, I just wanted to tell you how much I appreciate you and. . ."

"Scotty, you brought me into this league, tha. . ."

"Mac, shut up. What I wanted to tell you is that you're my second-favorite right winger to ever play for me. Next to Guy Lafleur. Hope you're not mad about that."

Not mad? For one of the few times in his life, Darren McCarty was speechless. "Oh no. No, not at all. Thank you Scotty," he finally said. "I just thank God my grandfather, Stormin' Norman Pritchard was there to witness it."

Now, when McCarty looks back on a roller-coaster of a career in hockey, he does so without a single regret. And he carries one colossal endorsement with him for all times.

"Dude, I'm good. People that know, *know*, and that's all that matters. I don't need any more flowers. When the greatest coach of all time tells me something like that? You know what? You don't have to be a Hall of Fame player to have a Hall of Fame moment. That's *my* Hall of Fame."

One unforgettable fight. One goal for the ages. And that

stamp of approval from Scotty Bowman? With that, Darren McCarty carved out his place among the most popular athletes in Detroit's history.

"He should be mayor of the city," Dave Lewis said. "Well, in a way, he already is."

The Trade

Doug MacLean was driving home from the airport feeling pretty good about life again. A few hours earlier, he had been unemployed with about $500 in the bank, his wife Jill pregnant with their daughter, and no health care. At that point, his best option was to return home to Canada, where childbirth costs wouldn't put him in massive debt.

Then his phone rang. At the other end of the line was his friend and professional mentor, Bryan Murray.

"How are you doing?" Murray asked.

"Really good," MacLean responded. "I just accepted a job to coach Philadelphia's farm club in Hershey."

"You've got to call them back and tell them you can't take the job."

"What? Why?

"Because you're coming to Detroit with me.

A week or so earlier, Murray and MacLean felt fairly confident that they were going to reunite in Philadelphia, but the Flyers had hired Russ Farwell as general manager instead. One of the National Hockey League's most successful coaches at the time, Murray had also made a strong impression when he interviewed with Mike

Ilitch in Detroit. Ilitch had decided to make some drastic changes after his team began to decline following two trips to the Western Conference finals under coach Jacques Demers in the late 1980s. Now the Red Wings were beginning to slide again, and the owner was out of patience.

He fired Demers and booted Jim Devellano upstairs to a new position as senior vice president. Now, eight years after hiring Devellano, Ilitch wanted new leadership. He hired Murray to fill both roles, general manager and coach. MacLean would be his associate coach.

When MacLean's plane landed at Detroit's Metropolitan Airport, Murray was there to meet him. On the way to their hotel, Murray dropped a bombshell.

"I've got some news," he said. "Sergei Fedorov has defected. He just arrived in Detroit."

And so began, that third week of July in 1990, the Murray and MacLean administration. And while it lasted less than five years, it had a profound impact on the dynasty the club was building as the team, the league and the entire world rambled headlong toward a new millennium.

In the pantheon of words written in articles and books, and stories on radio, TV, and on film, little has been said about how Murray and his staff helped to build the foundation of a team that would win three Stanley Cup titles in six seasons, and another one six years later. That changes now.

———————————

I first met Doug MacLean when he was a young coach with the St. Louis Blues, his first NHL gig as an assistant to coach Jacques Martin. In his two seasons there, MacLean did much of his work from the press box. He doubled as kind of Walmart greeter for visiting media, always with a smile and small talk during stoppages in play. Bespectled, with his dark hair perfectly manicured, he looked more like a middle school teacher grading homework with his notes spread out in front of him. Which is exactly what he was in life before hockey. Actually, life *between* hockey is probably more accurate.

When his playing career stalled, MacLean decided to return to the university—thanks in part to a scholarship recommendation from Bryan Murray—and get his teaching credentials. He returned home to Summerside, Prince Edward Island, and went to work in the classroom. Years later, in fact, when he found himself behind the Red Wings bench, there sat one of his former pupils, Gerard Gallant. But it was while earning his master's degree at the University of Western Ontario, in London, after seven years teaching in Summerside, that he got serious about coaching. During his master's studies, he worked as an assistant to Don Boyd, coach of the Ontario Hockey League's London Knights. On graduation, MacLean was appointed head coach at the University of New Brunswick. That was 1985. In his absolute must-read book, *Draft Day, How Hockey Teams Pick Winners or Get Left Behind* (Simon & Schuster, 2023), MacLean recalls taking his wife to dinner and explaining how the new head-coaching gig was the highlight of his life, and that he hoped to remain at UNB, "coaching hockey and teaching for the rest of my life."

Which lasted until the following spring. That's when Jacques Martin phoned to offer MacLean the assistant coaching job with the Blues. The university coach and professor took a $5,000 pay cut to hop aboard the NHL's volatile and unpredictable coaching carousel. The Blues gig lasted two years. But a day after Martin and MacLean were fired, MacLean got a call from another benefactor. Murray, then firmly entrenched as one of the most NHL's most successful coaches—at least in the regular season—was on the line offering MacLean a chance to interview for an assistant job with the Capitols.

It's difficult to imagine MacLean not getting any job for which he interviewed, given his engaging personality, combined with a quick mind, a sharp sense of humor and an easy, confident smile under which was a seething passion to succeed, to conquer whatever challenge confronting him. As it turned out, MacLean was the perfect yin to Murray's yang. MacLean never met a stranger. Murray, conversely, was more like the assistant principal you strived to avoid. Not that he was mean or intimidating. He just came across as more serious, reserved, cerebral, until he got to know you and a level of trust and respect was established. Then he'd unveil a softer side, immensely kind and sincere, with a dry sense of humor and a smile that amped up the room. And you'd come away feeling like he'd be as close to a friend as you can make despite a hard line separating journalist and source. That doesn't happen often.

I knew we had established something special when, a decade after Murray had left Detroit, we were filming the documentary, The Russian Five. By then, Murray was gravely ill, fighting stage 4 colon cancer that had begun to attack other organs in his body. I desperately wanted to get him in front of the camera, if only for a few minutes, to include him in our doc. After all, he was Sergei Fedorov's first coach. Same goes for Nick Lidstrom, Vladimir Konstantinov and Slava Kozlov. With such an influx of talent, it's little wonder the Wings started winning again—and this time the rest of the NHL was beginning to take notice.

I had tried for months to arrange an interview with Murray while he was still healthy enough. By then he was general manager of the Ottawa Senators, and his bad days were beginning to outnumber his good ones. Just before his team was to play the Wings at Joe Louis Arena, I got a call from Murray's assistant informing us that he would accompany his team to Detroit and be available for an interview. We set up the lights and camera in the lobby of his team's hotel, and when he came down I barely recognized him. He was a shadow of his former big, robust self, and I could sense he was nervous. So was I, until he flashed that smile.

It was painfully clear how important this moment was to Murray. He took great pride in his time in Detroit, as he well should have. He and MacLean, with assistant coach Dave Lewis, did wonders in developing all that young talent, which also included Martin Lapointe and Darren McCarty. But Murray was most enlightening when he described the young, anxious—and at times self-doubting—Fedorov. New country, new language, a very foreign style of hockey. Fedorov never doubted his own world-class talent. What worried him was if he'd ever really fit in. Murray sensed that and he spent an inordinate amount of time with his young superstar. In the process, they formed a powerful bond that manifested itself a decade later, when Fedorov left $10 million on the table to leave Detroit.

In a decision that I am certain haunts Fedorov to this day, he agreed to a four-year, $40 million deal with Anaheim, where Murray was the general manager, just days after Wings owner Mike Ilitch offered him $50 million over five years.

After about thirty minutes on camera, Murray looked exhausted, and I could tell by his eyes that he worried about whether he had given us what we needed. He certainly did; like every other of the hundreds of times I interviewed him, he was more than helpful. Sadly, far too much of what he shared with us wound up on the cutting room floor. In fact, he was left out of several early iterations of the film. But after more than a few major tantrums, I was able to convince the director and editors that they were guilty of an unconscionable oversight. Our film would be incomplete without

Bryan Murray sharing his thoughts about the early days of The Russian Five.

⬤————————⬤

By the time Murray and MacLean were aboard in Detroit, the 1990 draft had passed. Contrary to popular belief general managers have little influence on which players their teams select. Their job, primarily, is to ensure the chief scout and his staff have everything they need to evaluate the young prospects and select whichever ones are the best fit for the organization. If there is a debate at the draft table over who should be selected with the precious first-round pick, then the GM will weigh in. Either way, if a draft pick succeeds, it's the GM, more than the scouting staff, who gets the credit. Same goes for the blame, of course.

As the newly installed director of amateur scouting at the time, succeeding Neil Smith after he departed to run the New York Rangers, Ken Holland handled the 1990 draft with Jimmy Devellano, in his final days as GM before being succeeded by Murray. The Wings got two significant players: center Keith Primeau with the third overall selection and Slava Kozlov in the third round, forty-fifth overall. With Murray at the head of the draft table in 1991, Holland went four-for-four with their first four picks: power winger Martin Lapointe, tenth overall; defenseman Jamie Pushor in the second round, thirty-second overall; goaltender Chris Osgood in the third round, fifty-fourth overall; and right wing Mike Knuble in the fourth round, seventy-sixth overall. Six years later, all four would have their names engraved on the Stanley Cup after the Wings ended their forty-two-year drought.

In 1992, the Detroit Red Wings snagged just two NHL players, but both would have a profound impact on the Wings' future. To use a baseball analogy, Detroit struck out looking with their first-round pick, hit a grand-slam home run with their second selection, and arguably banged out a stand-up triple with their tenth rounder. The second-round selection was Darren McCarty, who played 758 games in the show, most of them in Detroit. The tenth-round pick was a big, rangy defenseman, Dan McGillis, who played 634 games with five clubs in the NHL, none of them in Detroit. (The other eight Detroit picks in that draft played a total of fourteen games in the NHL.) But McGillis turned out to be a valuable asset. He was the guy Scotty Bowman sent to Edmonton at the trade deadline in March 1996—for a guy named Kirk Maltby.

"I remember Glen Sather (then Edmonton's president and GM), calling us looking for a defenseman," Bowman said. McGillis was finishing up his college career at Northeastern University, and Detroit had little interest in signing him. "Edmonton said they were interested and gave us a choice of three players. We took Maltby."

So the Wings effectively wound up with two-thirds of their first incarnation of the Grind Line with what ordinarily would be described as a so-so draft in 1992. For the record, Maltby was Edmonton's third-round pick, sixty-fifth overall in that draft after scoring fifty goals in his final junior season. But he wasn't able to establish himself as a regular in the Oilers' lineup.

With the infusion of talent during Murray's tenure, the Wings became one of the more entertaining teams in the NHL. Led by their potent offense, they made the playoffs in each of Murray's three seasons behind the bench—but defensively they were generous to a fault, to describe it nicely. And goaltending remained the Achilles heel. By the spring of 1993, when Nikolai Borschevsky deflected a point shot by defenseman Bob Rouse past Detroit goaltender Tim Cheveldae at 2:35 of overtime in Game 7 to complete a shocking,

sickening first-round upset to the Toronto Maple Leafs, owner Mike
Ilitch had seen enough. He brought in Bowman to coach the club.

With another year on his contract, Murray kept his title as
general manager. MacLean was elevated from associate coach to
assistant general manager—his place behind the bench taken by
longtime Bowman sidekick Barry Smith. After nearly a decade on
the coaching carousel, MacLean was getting his first exposure to
life in an NHL front office—and he would make the most of it. A
big part of MacLean's new portfolio was managing the team's top
farm club, Adirondack.

"Doug was an ambitious young guy, a smart guy," Jim Devellano
recalled over dinner at his Florida home in February 2024. "And by
the way, he wrote a helluva book about the draft. But I remember
he was a very confident guy. Some people might say cocky, but I say
confident. I liked Doug because he was a worker."

MacLean knew if he put a good team together in Adirondack,
people would notice, So he beat the bushes looking for players who
could help his team win. And he found them, with a little help. In
what might be his greatest move in a front-office career that would
last more than two decades, MacLean acquired Kris Draper from
the Winnipeg Jets for next to nothing.

"Jimmy D. always tries to give me all the credit for Draper, and
I appreciate it," MacLean said in an interview from his home in
Prince Edward Island. "But Jim Clark was really the guy."

Clark, another Prince Edward Islander from Summerside, was a
part-time scout for the Wings, covering Eastern Canada. He'd been
following Draper's ascent for years, and when it appeared Draper's
career was stalling out in Winnipeg, Clark phoned MacLean.

"Doug, we've got to talk about this guy," MacLean recalled.
Draper had been sent back to the Jets' top AHL club in Moncton,
New Brunswick, and he wasn't happy.

"So really it was Jimmy Clark who was instrumental," said MacLean, who also well-aware of Draper's pedigree—third generation of elite players from one of the Toronto region's most-revered hockey families. "He like Kris Draper a lot, so I gave Mike Smith a call." The general manager of the Winnipeg Jets, Smith was in an unusually receptive mood when he picked up the phone.

"Mike was unbelievable," MacLean recalled. "He said, 'Doug, I love this kid, but my coach (John Paddock) won't play him. I'd love to do the kid a favor.'"

"Well, we'd like to have him," MacLean said, "so what can we do?"

Smith agreed to trade Kris Draper to Detroit for "future considerations."

"You know, Smith was a hard-ass guy, and he loved Kris Draper. That tells you all you need to know about Kris—and Mike Smith," MacLean said.

Except there was a hitch. The NHL vetoed the deal, ruling that there had to be something of value, more than the ambiguous "future considerations," going the other way for Draper to become a Detroit Red Wing.

"So we agreed on one dollar" to complete the paper transaction, MacLean said. In his book, MacLean said the return was a $1 US. But during our conversation in May 2024, MacLean was less certain about the return. "I'm pretty sure it was a Canadian dollar," he said. "I know I did give Mike Smith a dollar when I saw him."

Knowing MacLean as I do, and he remains among the most genuine people I've met in forty years covering the NHL, I'm sure he did what he said. I'm also willing to bet that the buck he paid Smith was a Canadian loonie, a coin just a bit smaller than an American silver dollar, featuring a loon on its front side. And if that's the case as I suspect, based on the exchange rate at the time, Detroit acquired the centerpiece of one of the most dominant checking lines in hockey history, a guy who went on to win four Stanley Cup rings, for seventy-two American cents.

A Very Canadian Story

In a conference room of the old Hyatt Regency Hotel in Dearborn, the newest Detroit Red Wing was smiling.

The exhaustive pre-camp physical exams were over, and athletic therapist John Wharton was announcing the top finishers in each event, including the bench press, vertical jump, pull-ups, hand strength, the dreaded one-mile run and the rather sadistic VO2 max, among others.

The same names kept cropping up in the top of nearly every event. The three young Russians—Sergei Fedorov, Vladimir Konstantinov and Slava Kozlov were all among the leaders in endurance events. Fedorov would always go last on pull-ups. He'd walk up to the bar and ask Wharton what the high number was. If Wharton said it was twenty-nine, Fedorov would do thirty and quit.

No one ever came close to Joe Kocur on the dynamometer, which measures hand strength —a reliable indicator of overall body strength, according to Wharton. In his encore performance with the Wings, Kocur would grip the machine until it screamed "Uncle!"

"I thought he broke it," Wharton said. "He'd always squeeze so hard he'd stick the needle at the end. I'd have to give it a shake so it came back to zero."

And then there was the VO2 max test—the gold standard for measuring aerobic fitness and universally loathed by even the fittest, world-class athletes for what it does to the body. Think being water-boarded by your own breakfast as it heads north in a desperate plea to tell the brain your body cannot produce another iota of oxygen needed to produce energy. VO2 max measures the volume of oxygen consumed per unit of time—how much oxygen you can take in, the ceiling, is your VO2.

The Russians owned that test until Wharton announced the name of the best-conditioned athlete in the Detroit Red Wings 1993 training camp. The winner of the team's Iron Man Award, complete with a plaque that adorned the wall in the team's weight room, was Kris Draper. Yeah, the new guy with the big grin on his face.

Who the hell is Kris Draper? Sure, he heard the whispers as he saw the other players looking around, his new teammates. At least he hoped these were his new teammates. This is exactly what he had hoped for in a long, grueling summer of preparation, intent on making a good first impression on the team that had rescued him from the scrap heap in Winnipeg the previous June 30.

Draper topped everyone in the room in the VO2 max test, finished third behind Konstantinov and Kozlov in the mile run, and distinguished himself in all the other categories as well. But the VO2 results were most impressive, Wharton said. The test is administered by having the subject ride a bike or run on a treadmill wearing a mask or breathing through a tube in their mouths with their nasal passages closed. The point of exhaustion, an indicator that the body has reached its maximum and is unable to produce any more energy, is where the data is extrapolated. Vomiting isn't necessary, but it happens.

Most of the best-conditioned Wings players that September tested in the high sixties to low seventies, Wharton said. Draper was alone in the high seventies. For comparison's sake, notorious bicy-clist Lance Armstrong tested at eighty-four at his peak, according to *topendsports.com*.

And Draper didn't step off the gas after making that strong first-impression. "He won our Iron Man the first two or three years he was with us," Wharton said. "He kind of helped me in a way. When he came in, he already had the foundation, working out like he did, He was in great physical condition right from the start of camp, which is what I was trying to build into our culture."

When Draper got to the rink the next day for the first practice of training camp, Wharton gave him another pat on the back. "You should be proud of that," Wharton said. And Draper was.

"I felt good about myself," he said. "I put in a lot that summer. I trained hard. I knew I was getting a fresh start, so I wanted to do well on all the tests—and I was at or near the top three in all of them. I thought I did everything I could to give myself an opportunity to get a pretty good look from the Detroit Red Wings management."

But testing well is one thing, and researchers are always quick to point out that tests like VO2 max are just an indication, not a reliable predictor, of performance. A center known for his blazing speed, Draper knew he had his work cut out for him to make the Detroit roster. Besides two eventual Hockey Hall of Famers ahead of him in Yzerman and Fedorov, the Wings boasted two other young centers chosen in the first rounds of their respective drafts—Mike Sillinger (eleventh overall in 1989—fifty-one picks ahead of Draper at sixty-second overall) and Keith Primeau (third overall in 1990). They were crowded up the middle, but Draper felt he'd earned at least an audition.

It didn't happen. After a few practices, with the first exhibition games looming, new Red Wings coach Scotty Bowman made his first round of cuts. Draper was stunned, outraged to be more precise, to see his name among them. He was assigned to Adirondack.

"That hit hard," Draper said. "I thought at least I'd get into a couple of exhibition games. I was pissed."

And his disappointment was palpable. Doug MacLean, who had such high hopes for Draper when he acquired him, now worried that the player was so angry that he might have second thoughts about reporting to the minors.

"I know Kris was really disappointed," MacLean said. "He had been beaten up to the point that we were worried he was contemplating not playing hockey anymore, that he'd just go back home to Toronto. I phoned Newell Brown and said, 'You'd better talk with this guy.' Honestly, I was nervous that he wasn't going to report."

Brown was in his second year behind the bench in Adirondack, and coincidentally he had some history with Draper. "He had actually recruited me for Michigan State when he was an assistant there to Ron Mason," Draper said. "We had a relationship all through my teenage years." The two had an earnest conversation in what turned out to be Draper's exit interview from Detroit's training camp. "He basically said, 'we're going to find that guy that I saw when I recruited you all those years," Draper said. "I told him I'd see him in Adirondack."

But he did detour slightly, spending a few days at home in suburban Toronto for what he called a much-needed reset. Bottom line, though, he stressed, he couldn't imagine any other option.

"There was never, ever a doubt that I wasn't going to Adirondack," he said. "Was I pissed off when I left Detroit? A hundred percent I was. And then you know what? That chip on my shoulder just got bigger. But honestly, I had no other options. I love the game too much. If there were seventy guys in training camp for the Detroit Red Wings that week, I know I loved the game more than sixty-nine of them. My love for the game runs deep. It still does, and it always will. So no, there wasn't a Plan B, even though when I left, it was like a dagger."

This was our lead-off topic in a long conversation at Embers Deli, a few blocks away from Oakland Hills Country Club, on a warm July afternoon in 2024. Earlier that day, Draper, a member of the club, had walked a few holes following Charlie Woods, Tiger's son, who was competing in the U.S. Junior Amateur. Draper arrived at the deli wearing a sweat-soaked T-shirt and shorts, both blue to match his sapphire eyes. His complexion glowed the way it did when he came off the ice after a hard practice. Entering his mid-fifties, he still maintained the physique—5-foot-10, 188 lean pounds—he had when he showed up in Detroit in his early 20s.

Draper had just come away from a fierce pickleball match, his latest in a lifelong string of athletic passions. We're talking serious pickleball. In fact, he said, the hockey rink in the backyard of his Bloomfield Hills home becomes a pickleball court as soon as weather permits. "It's a really great workout," he said. "The competition is real, and it can get pretty intense."

—————————

Kristopher Bruce Draper has lived his entire life with the kind of intensity most of us can only imagine. He was born into hockey royalty, three generations of prominent hockey men—now four since the Red Wings drafted Kienan Draper in 2020. Kris grew up in West Hill, Ontario, a neighborhood in the east end of Toronto, Canada's largest city. Also commonly called Scarborough, it's a culturally diverse, family oriented community where hockey is spoken year-around. And Kris Draper would have it no other way since the moment his father, Mike, first laced up Kris's skates and gently turned him loose on a sheet of ice located next to the house he grew up in—the house his parents own to this day.

"Honestly, it's a very Canadian story," he said. "We were the last house in a subdivision—we moved in when I was about 1 year old—and right beside our house was a pond. My dad didn't have to build a rink or anything. In those days, it would freeze over. I'd walk out the side door, and there it was. Mike Draper laced up his 3-year-old son's skates, gave him a nudge, and watched him take off. "I wouldn't come off the ice. I just loved it from the very beginning," Kris said. "Even just talking about it now puts a smile on my face. I probably had the snottiest nose a kid could have. The next year, when I was four, my dad put me in a league with six-year-olds—and I ended up playing.

The skating, especially the pace, the velocity in his stride, just seemed to come naturally. "Back then, there were no skating tread-mills or speed coaches," Draper recalled. "But if there was a rink, and obviously there was one right beside our house," I was on it." When he got a little older, the school nearby put up an outdoor rink every winter. "I'd come home from school, get all my homework done, then head out and skate for hours. It's just something I loved to do, and was pretty good at it, and it carried on throughout my whole career."

If anything, Draper credits genetics for what seemed to be natu-ral-born hockey skills.

Jack "Poppy" Draper, Kris's grandfather, was a defenseman who played minor pro hockey with the Pittsburgh Yellowjackets and the Toronto Goodyears in the 1930s. He had four sons, three of them prominent players as well. Mike Draper was a left wing who had a successful junior hockey career before attending Michigan Tech-nological University on Lake Superior in Houghton.

Twins Bruce and Dave seemed destined for even bigger things. Bruce was a left-shot center who played one game for the Toronto Maple Leafs before his career was cut short by cancer. He died at age twenty-seven. Kris never knew him, but the family always said Kris had Uncle Bruce's legs. Dave Draper was a winger who played with both brothers. With Bruce, he helped win the Memorial Cup with St. Michael's Majors in 1961. Later, with Mike, he played at Michigan Tech and helped win a national championship.

After his playing days, Uncle Dave became a junior coach and general manager, a college coach and, ultimately, one of the most respected NHL scouts in the history of the game. In fact, Dave was the chief scout of Colorado Avalanche, watching from the press box as his nephew crumpled to the ice after he was shoved ruthlessly from behind by Claude Lemieux, igniting one of the ugliest rivalries in NHL history.

Carrying on the family's rich hockey tradition was something that Draper did not take lightly. In his own pregame ritual, standing as the anthems were played, he would always think of his Poppy and the uncle he never met—along with his father and others who helped him get to the National Hockey League—and smile. Ironically, Poppy Draper died just a few days before that March 26, 1997 game at Joe Louis Arena, when the Wings finally had their revenge in that fight-filled victory the Colorado Avalanche.

"That was tough," Kris said, "a pretty emotional time for our family. But the way it turned out, I like to think it was Pops smiling down on that one."

Needless to say, when Kris encountered difficult decisions along his career path—and there would be several along his unusual, circuitous route to the National Hockey League—he never lacked for sound guidance and advice from well-informed sources.

Early on, Kris Draper could have lived happily ever after, at least through his formative years, playing hockey all day, every day. So he was in for a bit of a rude awakening as he packed up his equipment after his final game in his lone year of off-season youth hockey.

"So how did you enjoy playing summer hockey," he father asked.

"Dad, I loved it!"

"Well, I'm glad, because we'll never do this again?"

"But why?

"I'm not spending my summers in these rinks. So you know what? You're going to play tennis. You're going to play golf. You're going to play baseball."

More games. More competition. A young Kris Draper was just fine with that.

"I'm really glad I did," he said. "To this day, I still love to golf and play tennis, which has now transitioned to pickleball. I didn't just play hockey."

Draper played competitive tennis until he was 15. On the diamond, he spent his summers playing fastball, then baseball. Usually he played second base, but his favorite player growing up was Major League Baseball's all-star outfielder Rickey Henderson. "He was so fast, stole bases. I would always try to imitate him. I was a good runner, too, so I would always kid around. I'd say if I'm at first base, one pitch later I'll be on second. See you later."

Draper attended De La Salle College, a prep school in Toronto, and though he enjoyed competing in other sports, hockey remained is passion and his No. 1 priority. It became his full-time vocation when he turned 16 and was drafted in the fourth round by the Windsor Spitfires of the 1988 OHL Priority Selection. Now he had two traditional options: play major junior hockey or, when he graduated, play for Spartans at MSU, an annual powerhouse during the tenure of renowned coach Ron Mason. But Draper, largely on the advice of his family, chose a third path after he was invited to play for Team Canada – an honor (and a long shot) at such a tender age.

"I mean, why wouldn't I go, right?" he asked. "They invited a handful of teenagers, minor pro guys and some guys out of Europe and the American (Hockey) League to put this development team together and get ready for the 1992 Olympics."

The week-long camp was in Calgary, a moon-shot away for a kid who had never been out of Eastern Canada. Draper survived several early cuts. He figured his turn came when coaches Dave King and Guy Charron called him in for a meeting after a practice late in the week.

"Kris, we've enjoyed seeing what you've been doing here," King said, "and we'd love for you to be part of Team Canada as we start building for the Olympics."

Draper was shocked. He'd never been to Western Canada before, and now, if he accepted this invitation, it would be home. So he talked it over with his family. Junior hockey? U.S. college hockey? Or Team Canada? It was Uncle Dave who drove the most important point home: The chance to play alongside some of Canada's best amateur players under two of the country's finest coaches was impossible to pass up.

"There's really no decision to make here," Dave Draper said. "This is a terrific opportunity for you."

So off he went to Calgary, playing for two seasons and, remarkably, preserving his amateur status that kept him eligible for U.S. college hockey as well as major junior hockey. As an 18-year-old, he was drafted by Winnipeg and ended up making Canada's world junior team, winning gold with his defensive prowess that helped put a blanket over Soviet star Pavel Bure. Again, though, Draper found himself at a crossroads with the Olympics still eighteen months away. By then, he had an agent, Don Meehan, who helped him sort out his options, which became more complicated with rumors that the NHL may release its players to compete in the 1992 Winter Games. Draper wanted a guarantee that he would be part of the team even if NHL players were invited to compete. Coach Dave King couldn't make that promise. So Draper was back to considering his other options. Now, however, along with college hockey and major juniors, the NHL was in the mix and calling. Meehan advised his client that Winnipeg was interested in signing him.

Ultimately, Draper set aside his dream of representing his country in the Olympics and signed with the Jets, figuring he'd be in camp for a week and then, like most 18-year-olds in NHL training camps, be reassigned to a junior club. But a week passed, and then another. And every day he came to the rink, there was a jersey hanging in his stall. Then he got called into a meeting with GM John Ferguson and coach Bob Murdoch, figuring this was the end of the road for him. As he remembered the moment, sitting at an outdoor table at a West Bloomfield deli sipping on a hot cup of coffee on a humid July afternoon, Kris Draper was overtaken by chills.

"Congratulations Kris," Ferguson said. "You're going to be on the opening-night roster."

"Oh my. . ." Draper responded in one of the few times in his life that he was caught speechless. "I kinda shocked the world."

Sure enough, opening-night in Winnipeg and Draper was in the lineup against his hometown Toronto Maple Leafs. And what an auspicious debut. He scored a goal, got into a fight—two thirds of a Gordie Howe hat trick—and was named the third star of the hockey game. But he also wound up on the injured list. In the fight against Drake Berehowsky, a big defenseman he grew up with in Toronto, Draper sprained ligaments in his ankle when the combatants tumbled to the ice with the linesman. He ended up missing five weeks. When he was ready to play again, the Jets sent him to Moncton, New Brunswick for a two-week conditioning stint in the American Hockey League. He scored a goal in his first game there, too.

When Draper was recalled to Winnipeg, he joined a very different Jets team. "Winnipeg was just a gong show, and right away I got called in to talk with Bob and Fergie," Draper recalled. "They both said they didn't expect to make it through the season, so they were sending me down to Ottawa, in the Ontario Hockey League, to play for the great coach Brian Kilrae." For the second straight year, Draper would represent Canada on its world junior team. Even better, he said, "Saskatoon was hosting the tournament, right there in Canada."

So Draper wound up wearing four different sweaters in the 1990-91 season—but that's not what made him the answer to a unique trivia question. As he was prone to doing, he scored a goal in his first game for Ottawa, too. So here's the question: who's the only player ever to score his first NHL goal before his first AHL goal and his first AHL goal before his first OHL goal—all three goals coming in the first game he played in those leagues? Yeah, it's Kris Draper. Even better, he won his second World Junior Championship, again helping to shut down Bure and his electric Soviet teammate, Slava Kozlov.

When Draper showed up in Winnipeg's training camp to start the 1991-92 season, Bob Murdoch was the new coach and Mike Smith was the general manager. Training camps are hard enough on young players, but having to impress a new regime—one that didn't draft them—added a whole new layer of pressure. But again, Draper heard those magical words near the end of Winnipeg's training camp: find a place to live, you're staying put.

"I ended up rooming with Keith Tkachuk," Draper said. "Actually, I might have spent one night in my apartment. They ended up sending me back to Moncton anyway."

That's how it would be for the next two seasons. Up and down, mostly down in the minors, which led to the Draper family burning up the phone lines to and from Toronto. Always, Draper's father was there to help talk him off the ledge.

"You start to question yourself, wonder if you can actually make it a career in the NHL," he said. "My dad was just always there, always keeping me positive. He told me I could only control what I can control, so just go out and work hard in practice—and after practice. And if you get an opportunity, take advantage of it. Mike Draper saw enough of his son those two years Kris helped Canada win gold in World Juniors—best-on-best among the greatest hockey-playing nations in the world—to know his son was good enough to compete in the NHL, that he just needed that opportunity. "My dad was a big part of me not losing confidence," Kris said.

Still, it wasn't easy. He played just seventeen more NHL games over those two seasons with the hapless Jets. In that time, playing limited minutes, he scored two goals. His time in the minors was much more productive, which is why *The Hockey News* listed Draper third among the Jets' top prospects behind Stu Barnes and Russ Romaniuk. Apparently, Winnipeg didn't get the memo. When Moncton's season ended early, the Jets recalled several players to beef up their taxi squad. Kris Draper was not among them.

Time to have another chat with his agent.

"Donnie, it seems like this isn't a fit for me," a dejected Draper told Meehan. "Obviously, I'll go back to Moncton if that's what I have to do, but I know I can play."

"Well, let's see what we can do," Meehan responded.

And on the last day of June, four days after the 1993 NHL draft in Quebec City, Draper was traded to Detroit. "For the old 'Freddie Charles,'" Draper said, meaning FC—future considerations. Which turned out to be a buck. Now his struggle to find his place in the National Hockey League began all over again.

Despite winning the Iron Man award in his first camp with Detroit, it would have been shocking for Draper to have made the Detroit roster. Had he earned at least an audition with an exhibition game or two? Absolutely, but there were important mitigating circumstances. NHL coaches are notorious for wanting to pare their training camp rosters down to what they expect will be their Opening Night rosters as quickly as possible. And this was especially important for Bowman, coming into the job facing enormous expectations by a fan base that had been beaten up for nearly four decades. Bowman needed those exhibition games to take a long, hard look at his other young centers, Primeau, Sillinger and Greg Johnson.

Besides, and this sounds harsh in retrospect, MacLean had his own plans for the minor league club he was running. "To be perfectly honest," he said, "I wasn't even thinking NHL when we traded for Draper. I was trying to build something in Adirondack, put a good team there."

That summer, MacLean also signed free agent Tim Taylor, a center who had played for him years earlier in Baltimore of the AHL. MacLean was counting on Draper and Taylor to center the team's top two lines. And it worked. Despite the early turbulence with Detroit, Draper, along with Taylor got off to a blazing start in Glens Falls. "Kris and Timmy Taylor were on fire from the opening drop of the puck—an unbelievable start to the season, even though a couple other of our young guys, Darren McCarty and Martin Lapointe, were really struggling," MacLean said. "But overall we had a special group of players there in Adirondack, and that helped Drapes."

Back in Detroit, Scotty Bowman was intrigued by the reports he was getting, particularly about Draper, but Taylor as well to some respect. In January, about halfway through the season, Bowman accompanied Murray, MacLean and Holland to see the Adirondack club play at the Hamilton Coliseum. It was as close to love at first sight as it gets between coach and player.

"Scotty was drooling over Draper," MacLean recalled, "and you know what a hardass Scotty was."

Bowman was impressed for good reason. Draper played one of the best games ever in what was turning out to be his best professional season to date. And coincidentally, since Hamilton is just a short drive down the road from Toronto, his parents and several other family members and friends were on hand to see it. After the game, a beaming Kris Draper was standing outside the dressing room talking with his father when Bowman walked up. He addressed Mike Draper first (because Bowman knows everybody in hockey), then he turned to Kris.

"You played well tonight," Bowman said. Draper smiled. "Face-offs!"Bowman added. "Do you know how you did on face-offs tonight?"

Draper shrugged. "I felt like I had I had a pretty good night," he said. But there was no empirical evidence. That stat wasn't on the final game summary in those days, even in the NHL.

"Kris, you won nineteen of twenty-one tonight. No one wins draws like that in Detroit. Can you do that in the NHL?"

"Yes I can, Scotty." Draper was now beaming.

"Then the craziest thing happens," Draper said. "He just walks away, as Scotty does, and as he's leaving he says, 'We'll see you in about two weeks.' And I'm standing there like, what's that supposed to mean? Is he coming down to see me again in Adirondack in two week, or am I coming up to him?"

Turns out, Bowman had seen enough. Jimmy Devellano recalls the conversation he had about Draper after the coach and Holland returned from Hamilton. "The kid can skate, and he wins face-offs," Bowman said. "I don't know if he has any hands or not, but I think he can help us."

Draper laughed when I mentioned the coach's thumbnail scouting report. "I have a little bit of a different story than Scotty has," Draper said. "That night he came to Hamilton? I had a hat trick.

And he never mentioned it. The three goals, that didn't do anything for him. He had guys who could score goals. I knew that, and I also knew why I had a good chance of getting called up.

Face-offs. Widely overlooked by the average fan, the battle for the puck when it's dropped on the dot by an official is vitally important because success or failure at that moment can have a dramatic affect on the game's outcome. The average NHL game has between fifty and seventy face-offs, and each one will result in one team gaining possession of the puck. The more face-offs won, the greater opportunity to control the puck, the greater the opportunity to generate more shots, more and better scoring changes and potentially the goal or two that separates a win from a loss. Coaches like Bowman spend sleepless nights devising strategies and scoring options after winning an offensive zone face-off because it's a huge tactical advantage. But first, their centers have to win the draw, a skill Draper had been developing since his earliest days as a teenager with Team Canada.

"I was seventeen-eighteen years old and playing against the Soviet Red Army and guys like Krutov, Larionov and Makarov—those guys," Draper said, naming one of the greatest forward lines in the history of the game. "And I remember our assistant coach, Guy Charron, kind of warning me: 'If you don't win a face-off, you won't see the puck the entire shift.' And I'm like, that kind of makes sense. So all I'm thinking about is the importance of face-offs. It was that simple."

Throughout his two-plus years with the national team, Draper worked on draws—along with so many other elements of the game often overlooked by younger players. "Most guys that age are working on the offensive side of the puck, working the power play, playing twenty-five minutes a night and scoring goals. I was doing the exact opposite. I was getting taught the defensive side of the game.

I had to check. I had to be responsible. I could always skate. That was always an asset that I had. But I had to learn to play in my own end, learn how to kill penalties. I was taught at a young age how to play without the puck because our teams were so overmatched when we played internationally.

"So that's where I learned the importance of face-offs. And as crazy as it sounds, that one good night in Hamilton, and Scotty was there and I win a lot of face-offs, that got me my opportunity in Detroit."

Ironically, the opportunity opened up for him when Greg Johnson—who was having a hard time cracking Bowman's lineup—joined Team Canada in hopes of playing in the 1994 Olympics. It was time, finally, for Draper to get his audition in Detroit. That trip to Hamilton was the first and only time Bowman had seen Draper play before summoning him.

"January 23, 1994, I got the call up to Detroit," Draper recalled. Two nights later, he made his Red Wings debut in a 5-0 loss to Chicago at Joe Louis Arena. He announced his presence with seventeen penalty minutes in that game—two minutes for charging in the first period and a high-sticking major on defenseman Steve Smith along with a game-misconduct penalty with fifteen seconds remaining in the game. Two nights later, in Chicago, the Wings won, 4-3, in overtime. It was another typically ornery tussle between the two Original Six rivals, but this time Draper stayed out of the penalty box while recording his first point for Detroit, an assist on a goal by Martin Lapointe, his linemate in Adirondack just a few weeks earlier.

Now that he was back in the NHL, Draper's mission was to stay for awhile. To do that, he relied on the advice of his longtime personal trainers, John and Peter Renzetti, who not only helped Draper stay in superb physical condition year around but also instilled a mindset that shaped his work ethic.

"We've got to make you the hardest-working guy in the NHL," said Peter Renzetti, who later spent several seasons as the strength and conditioning coach for the Detroit Red Wings.

"I'm in," Draper said. "One part of it was coming into camp in very good shape. I was physically strong. Then the mindset came: I have to be relentless. Every day I came to the rink with the attitude that no one is taking my fucking job."

A little superstition never hurt either. Before his first game with the Wings, Draper approached athletic therapist John Wharton about getting some legwork in before the game. His legs contributed to the most important part of his game, speed, and he liked to include a brief massage of his calves and thighs as part of his pregame ritual. Wharton of course accommodated him, and when Draper's sweater was in his stall before his second game, he approached Wharton again.

"It became kind of a ritual as one game turned into two, and two games turned into three," Wharton recalled. "He didn't know how long he would stay, but we were both hoping it would work out. So before every game he'd come in and say, 'Johnny, can we tickle the moneymakers?' And he'd get a little leg massage. I think we stopped counting when Game 37 turned into Game 38."

Kris Draper, of course, never saw the minors again. He played until he was forty. And he didn't want to quit even then. As he got older, he paid more attention to his nutrition. He took care of himself physically, continuing his daily workout routine even through the off-season, much like his father still did at age eighty-five. And the legs, those magnificent moneymakers, were still doing their thing.

"I felt that if I could skate, I could continue to play," he said. The Wings, however, thought otherwise. After seventeen seasons with Draper, they appeared to be moving on. The best they could do was offer him a two-way deal; if he didn't make the NHL roster, he would draw a minor-league salary in Grand Rapids. The writing was on the wall.

"I was forty years old, and obviously I would have loved to keep playing, but as we all know, Father Time is undefeated," he said. Oh, his prospects were much better of signing a one-year, hanger-on deal with another NHL club, but did he really want to uproot his young family and move them to another city, a new, likely temporary home, new schools, all that? "It was something that I wrestled with pretty hard, but I realized that would have been very selfish of me, considering all the sacrifices my wife made, that my kids made. I just felt it was time to walk away from the game. But it wasn't easy.

"There are a lot of guys, some really good players, who when they walk away they're done with it. They don't miss it at all. I was the exact opposite."

By the time he announced his retirement at an 11 a.m. news conference on July 26, 2011, Kris Draper was one of the most accomplished players ever to wear the winged wheel. All but twenty of his 1,157 NHL games were with the Red Wings. He was the fifth player ever to play 1,000 games with Detroit. He ranked ninth all-time in the NHL with 222 Stanley Cup playoff games when he retired.

Starting in 1997-98, Draper won at least fifty-two percent of his face-offs in each of his final thirteen NHL seasons, one of the finest runs of success in the circle in the NHL. Centering the Grind Line in a largely defensive role, Draper helped Detroit win back-to-back Stanley Cup titles in 1997-98, then he added some offense to his arsenal. He scored fifteen goals in 2001-02, when the Wings sent Scotty Bowman into retirement with another Stanley Cup ring. And in 2003-04, Draper had a career-high twenty-four goals—and won the Selke Trophy as the NHL's best defensive forward. He won a fourth Stanley Cup in 2008 in an encore performance for The Grind Line, adding more bling to his luminous resume.

On the day Draper announced his retirement, General Manager Ken Holland announced that he wasn't going anywhere, that Draper would be joining the front-office staff as a special assistant. Draper then began the long process of learning the inner-workings of an NHL front office. His tutelage would be very similar to what Steve Yzerman experienced when he retired in 2006. Yzerman's ascension in the organization, however, was much more immediate. Three months after his retirement, the former captain was named vice president and alternate governor. Regardless of titles, though, Yzerman had as much to learn as Draper in their first days in the front office.

"I was officially special assistant, and then I asked Ken if we could drop the 'special,'" Draper told reporters at the time. "Ken was very gracious with the title. I wasn't in charge of anything, really. I just went and watched hockey games and put reports in. I don't know if anybody read them. That was the role there. But to be able to walk out of the Detroit Red Wings (dressing) room and into the Detroit Red Wings front office was something that Ken gave me, that opportunity, and that's a big reasons I'm sitting here now."

Yzerman, of course, left Detroit's executive staff in 2010 to become general manager of Tampa Bay, where he helped to build a Lightning team that would eventually win back-to-back titles after his resignation. He returned to Detroit as executive vice president and general manager on April 19, 2019, and eventually elevated Draper to director of amateur scouting and one of two assistant managers, with Shawn Horcoff.

And thirty-one years later, and counting, Kris Draper continues to live his best life with the Detroit Red Wings. Not a bad deal for the Wings in that long-ago deal with Winnipeg—even if it cost them an American buck.

A brief foot-note: Tim Taylor was also recalled to Detroit, joining Draper in that 1993-94 season. In the only game he played for the Wings that season, his NHL debut, Taylor scored a goal. The following year, he made the club in Detroit, the first of three seasons with the Wings. In 1997, he and Draper were Stanley Cup champion teammates. Taylor would play 746 games with four teams over twelve NHL seasons, culminating in 2006-07, when he served as captain of the Tampa Bay Lightning. Entering the 2024-25 season, he was an assistant general manager with the St. Louis Blues.

After helping the Wings acquire Draper, Jim Clark was rewarded with a nice promotion. MacLean hired him as the director of hockey operations in Adirondack in 1993. Clark left the Red Wings organization in 1996 to join Murray and MacLean with the Florida Panthers. In 1998, when MacLean was named president and general manager of the expansion Columbus Blue Jackets, he hired Clark again, this time to serve as vice president and assistant general manager, roles he performed for ten years. Clark joined the Ottawa Senators as a scout in 2008, and in 2014 he was promoted—by then GM Bryan Murray—to director of professional scouting, a position he still held ten years later.

What Am I Doing Here?

Ten-year-old Landon Maltby sat across the restaurant table in yet another Midwestern town hosting yet another travel hockey tournament, making small talk between games with his famous father. As usual, Dad was extolling the virtues of winning hockey: playing responsibly defensively, killing penalties, blocking shots—none of it much fun for kids. During a pause in their conversation, Landon asked a question that stopped his father in mid-bite.

On the small size for his age group—he wouldn't catch up for another five years or so when he would sprout eight inches in a ten-month span—Landon was wise beyond his years, as his question suggested.

"Dad, when did it occur to you—when did you *know*—that you had made in hockey?"

Seemed like a question that, if it was pass across a patch of ice, Kirk Maltby could have slapped into an open net. Yet he had no idea how to answer it. If he could at all.

Landon and his fraternal twin sister, Leighton, were born two years before their father retired. But of course, by the time he had posed that question, Landon knew much about his dad's career thanks to the all-knowing internet. It's all right there on the fingertips; click on "Kirk Maltby highlights" on YouTube and the first clip available—a minute and thirty-eight seconds long—shows all that's necessary to know about what kind of player Landon's dad was: "Kirk Maltby blocks three shots without a stick." Indisputable evidence showing what it takes to win when it mattered most.

That was Game 5 of the 2002 Stanley Cup Western Conference Semifinals. The Wings were killing a penalty with Maltby and Kris Draper up front and Nick Lidstrom and Chris Chelios on defense trying to protect a 1-0 lead at Joe Louis Arena. Maltby lost his stick early in the shift, and the Blues had sustained pressure cycling the puck in the Detroit zone. Not once, but three times Maltby threw his body in front of pucks headed toward the Detroit net—all hard slapshots from the point. Two were by Alexander Khavanov and the other by Al MacInnis, owner of one of the most lethal shots in the history of the league. Step in front of one of his shots, you'd better have your life insurance premiums up to date. But there was Maltby, doing what he did best, which was anything and everything to help his team win. A Joe Louis Arena crowd on its feet cheering wildly as Maltby gingerly made his way to the bench didn't lessen the pain, but it sure made him feel appreciated. Just keep the ice packs coming.

Among plenty of other such highlights for Landon and his pals to watch: Kirk Maltby's lone NHL hat trick in a lopsided win at Toronto—forty-five minutes from where he grew up in Hespeler Village, Ontario—on December 27, 1997, a series of thunderous hits, and more than a few scraps, including a memorable one. He fought Colorado's Rene Corbet on the undercard of the most iconic game in the 98-year history of the Detroit Red Wings on March 26, 1997.

So when did you know, Dad?

When indeed.

It might have been when the Edmonton Oilers drafted him in the third round (sixty-fifth overall) in the 1992 National Hockey League Entry Draft. But then he showed up for training camp, a guy who had scored fifty goals in his final season in junior hockey with the Owen Sound Platers. It was his first truly rude awakening in the game: goals are infinitely harder to come by at the professional level. He knew he'd have to round out his game to survive in the NHL. And players like him, he learned realized, measured their survival shift by shift by shift.

It might have been in his first-ever NHL game with the Edmonton Oilers at the old Boston Garden. Maltby was a nervous, wide-eyed rookie sitting on the bench when, just moments before the game, he noticed a friendly face on the ice. One of Maltby's closest, lifelong friends in Hespeler was Shawn Hodges, whose father, Bob, was an NHL official—one of the most respected linesmen in the game. Hodges worked 1,701 regular-season games and 157 playoff games in a twenty-six-year career, and one of those was at Boston Garden that night, where his son's pal was making his big-league debut.

"Hi Mr. Hodges!" Maltby said, as the linesman skated by. After a quick circle, Hodges skated back over to the Edmonton bench, winked at Maltby and whispered, "Call me Bob." Maltby understood then that he was experiencing some kind of transition in his life, but still he wasn't feeling remotely like he'd made it.

So when? Maltby kept asking himself, trying to give his son a serious response to a thoughtful, serious question.

It might have been when he was still in Edmonton, playing the visiting Detroit Red Wings, when he lined up a Wings defenseman for a hit that would have put him in the third row were it not for the Plexiglas separating players and patrons.

"He almost killed Paul Coffey with a bodycheck," former Wings coach Dave Lewis said. Lewis was an assistant to Scotty Bowman then, and he distinctly remembers Bowman's reaction, the famous coach with an almost imperceptible nod and a raised eyebrow that spoke volumes. As auditions go, that hit was as good as it gets. "It opened Scotty's eyes," Lewis said. "Now Kirk Maltby was on Scotty's radar." When it came to hockey, the coach had a photographic memory. And here was an indelible, foreshadowing moment in Maltby's NHL career, though he had no idea about it at the time.

"I do remember the hit," Maltby said. "I got the best of him, but thinking back, I wonder how the hell I did it considering what a great skater Paul Coffey was." After the hit, however, Maltby admitted to spending the rest of the game looking over his shoulder. "All I could think about was where's Bob Probert or (Darren) McCarty or (Martin) Lapointe? Who's coming after me."

But Maltby survived the game and afterward joined some Oilers teammates at Barry T's, an Edmonton nightclub (the '90s version of the infamous Goose Loonies in the '80s) for a few cold ones. The Wings were staying over, and some of them wound up at the same club. Among them was Coffey, who made a beeline for Maltby as soon as he spotted him.

"I'd never met Paul in my entire life," Maltby said. "But he came over, put his arm around me and said, "Kid, don't ever hit me like that again." Then they laughed about it, bought each other a beer and called it a night. That's the rather "modern" National Hockey League. What happens on the ice stays there. Rarely do things carry over off the ice—unlike the days of train travel, when rivalries were fierce, opposing teams would shuttle together between Original Six cities and confrontations in the Club Car were common. Now, here was a future Hockey Hall of Famer and a kid struggling to stay in the league, just a couple of hockey guys enjoying an adult beverage after a hard day's night.

So, was there ever a time when Kirk Maltby felt he had actually made it, that he belonged, that he felt deserving and comfortable among world's most talented hockey players in the best league on the planet? All those moments flashed through his mind as his son sat across the table waiting for a response that would eventually surface.

———

By his own account, Kirk Maltby enjoyed a rather modest, tranquil childhood in Hespeler, one of three close-knit communities that comprise the greater Cambridge, Ontario. The other two are Preston and Galt. The three cities were amalgamated in 1973, a year after Maltby was born, but the folks in Hespeler retain a certain sense of pride in their community—perhaps with a little bit of attitude.

"People in Preston usually just say they're from Cambridge, and the people in Galt also usually say they're from Cambridge," Maltby said. "But people in Hespeler always say they're from Hespeler."

Purchased in 1798 by a group of Pennsylvania Mennonites from the Six Nations Indians, the region that became known as Hespeler is located on the Speed River in Southwest Ontario. Today Hespeler Village boasts a population of about 26,000 souls—the vast majority of them, like all of Canada, obsessed with hockey. Not only do they take pride in being the birthplace of NHL stars like four-time Stanley Cup champion Kirk Maltby and former Red Wings captain-turned-broadcaster Paul Woods, they can be quick to mention that Hespeler Wood Specialty Company factories once turned out more hockey sticks than anywhere in the world. The company was later owned by Canadian Tire—where most young hockey players bought their first sticks ("$19.99 before taxes," Maltby recalls). More recently, it was owned by sporting equipment manufacturer

Cooper Canada, which ultimately was acquired by Bauer Hockey when the giant skatemaker diversified its product line. But whoever controlled the company was still making sticks when Maltby was a youngster, which generously contributed to his blissful upbringing.

"From the time I was about five until I left to go play junior hockey, we had a backyard, and behind the yard was a wooded area," Maltby said. "And behind those woods. . ."

Ah, behind those woods was a young athlete's version of Willy Wonka's Chocolate Factory.

"Behind those woods was the Bauer-Cooper plant where they made baseball bats and hockey sticks," Maltby explained. "They would have a lot of rejects, things that weren't quite right with the bats and sticks. And there was this big huge firewood pile of stuff they were just throwing away. So as kids we'd just go through the woods, grab some things and come back and play baseball or road hockey or ministicks."

Rather idyllic for the first-born son of Sue and Fred Maltby, both factory workers who worked the 7 a.m.-3 p.m. shift five days a week and enjoyed frequent family gatherings on the weekends. Horseshoes was the game. The men played it. The women played it. Even the kids played it. Family tournaments. Serious horseshoes.

"I'm not sure if idyllic is the right word, but certainly those were simpler times. No internet. No cell phones. No hand-held games. We were a blue-collar family. We didn't have a lot of extra money to spend. We still had a rotary phone when everyone else had pushbuttons."

Brother Shawn, four years younger, got all the hand-me-down hockey equipment. Kirk's secondhand gear came from a kid down the street—same age but always a little bigger. The one thing the Maltby boys got new when they needed them was protective cups.

So the Bauer-Cooper fire pit behind the woods was a bit of a

Godsend for boys who spent their summers on the diamonds playing baseball and winters on whatever ice they could find to play hockey. And as much as their sons were consumed by hockey, Maltby's parents insisted their boys play both sports.

"I wanted to play hockey so badly, especially in the summer when my friends would be going to summer camps. But my mom and dad would say, 'Nope, you play hockey in the winter and you play baseball in the summer.'"

So when the buzzer sounded on the last playoff hockey game in the spring, the equipment bag would get zipped up and it was all baseball from there. And by baseball, Maltby was referring to "fastball," as it's referred to throughout Canada, especially in its smaller communities. The game is known more as fast-pitch softball in the United States, where it is typically now played mostly by girls and women. In church leagues and rec leagues throughout Canada, fastball is enormously popular and played by anyone who enjoys the challenge of trying to hit a 70 mph (baseball's equivalent of 90 mph) ball coming from the pitcher's circle just 46-feet away. Canadians are good at that, too, perennially boasting some of the most dominant men's and women's teams in the world.

"At a really young age, I was one of the pitchers," Maltby said, "but one day we didn't have a catcher, so I thought I'd try that—and I loved it. For five or six years, I played catcher. We had a really good travel softball team, and our church league was unbelievable.

"I'm glad my parents didn't let me play just hockey for twelve months a year—as much as I wanted to. Baseball was a big part of my development, with things like eye-hand coordination. I think it's really important that kids play more than one sport."

(Which may explain why all his children are multi-sport athletes. His oldest daughter, Ella, is a two-sport athlete in college, playing volleyball and lacrosse. Landon plays travel hockey and lacrosse, and he loves competitive tennis and swimming. His twin sister Leighton is an elite-level gymnast for her age group and also a competitive swimmer.)

As much as he enjoyed fastball, however, Maltby was madly in love with skating and hockey from the moment he took his first strides on a pair of blades on a flooded rink in a neighbor's back yard. Jeff Pelley was a neighborhood friend, and Jeff's dad, Gerald, built a little twelve-foot-square sheet of ice. "That's where I learned to skate," Maltby said, "and after that it was nothing but skating, skating, skating. It wasn't very big, but we made the most of it."

When he was ready for a bigger ice surface and a challenge with a stick and a puck, there were a couple of rinks in a park just four doors away from his family's home. There were two baseball diamonds at the park, but once winter came to stay, the local fire department would flood them and create two rinks, one on each ball field.

"Oh, we had so many kids come out to play in the cold," he said. "We would leave the nets and shovels and everything there, and whoever showed up first would shovel the snow off, and we'd basically have one rink for hockey and the other rink for everyone else who just wanted to skate."

So began a pattern of life he enjoyed for several years: home from school, straight to the rink, back home for a quick dinner, back to the rink until it was time clean up and head to bed.

"All winter, I was either on the ice with whichever team I was playing for, or I was on the ice with my friends at the park," he said. It wasn't until he was about fifteen, when it occurred to him and his parents that he might have an opportunity to play elite-level hockey, that his parents finally relented and said, "OK, you can play summer-league hockey, too."

Now things were getting serious. Playing well and winning were becoming more important. And Maltby was getting serious about the game. While he never had problems with his temper, there was one time when it got the best of him, to his dismay. It happened near the end of a game and he was on the ice when the opponents scored what turned out to be the winning goal. In a flash of anger, Maltby slammed his twenty-dollar hockey stick over the crossbar of the goaltender's cage, breaking it into pieces.

"My parents saw what happened," he said. And when he walked out to the car carrying just one stick, he got an earful from his mom—that age-old parental lecture about how money doesn't grow on trees.

But as excited as Maltby was about how his game was developing—he was an exceptional skater who had begun to show some skills with the puck—he experienced mixed feelings about the uncertainties ahead. He had reached a crossroad after a successful Bantam season. What next? "Do I go play Midget hockey or try out for the local Junior B team?" he wondered. He got his answer when several of his friends decided to try out for the Junior team. "So that's what I did."

Practices were intense. There were cuts, and some of his friends were sent packing. More cuts and more friends gone. "Cuts got made, and I was still there. More cuts made, and I was still there," he said. "I remember talking to one of my best buddies and saying to him, 'even if I make the team, I'm not going to play. I would rather play with you guys, my buddies, my friends.'"

But Maltby persevered, and, after much deliberation, he signed on with the Junior B Cambridge Winter Hawks. "I made it, but I didn't know anybody. It was a real eye-opener. My whole life I had coaches that I knew. Now I've got a coach I had never met, and he was a hard ass. He was stern, and I wasn't used to it."

That he was always one of the better players on his minor hockey teams meant nothing to this new coach, the late Mike Kearns. Maltby was barely sixteen playing against twenty-year-olds, and he was right about not getting as much playing time as he did when he was younger. Naturally, there were some second thoughts. "Not that I wanted to quit," he confessed, "but I did stop and ask myself: 'Damn, what am I doing?'"

Turned out, the answer to that question amazed even him. As the season progressed, Maltby began to find his stride, playing well, producing points and even making the league's all-star team. "I have to give credit to my coach there," he said. "He stuck with me even when I had some doubts."

While he wasn't making a dime playing Junior B hockey, Maltby got a kick out of the fact that people were charged admission to watch his team play at the 720-seat Hespeler Memorial Arena. Well, not everybody. "I'd mention to my friends that I had a game," Maltby recalled, and they'd say, 'We're not paying five bucks to go see that!' But it was really kind of cool that people were actually paying for tickets to come watch us play."

Hespeler's hockey community was tiny by Canadian standards, and its Junior B team was often overmatched by several power-houses in the province. "We were often just happy we could keep the score in single digits," Maltby said. Nevertheless, he was beginning to attract attention. Agents started calling. Various major junior teams were wanting to talk to him.

"The OHL was coming into play," he said. "I knew who the Kitchener Rangers were. I knew about the Guelph Platers. But I had never even seen a (major) junior game in my life. I'm still living at home. If I get drafted, where am I going to play? Am I going to have to move away from home?"

It was all a bit overwhelming for a small-town kid, but for a moment it looked like he could make it work comfortably. He was drafted by Guelph. The Maltby home in Hespeler to the 3,999-seat Guelph Memorial Gardens was 20-25 minutes by car, tops. He could live at home and get rides from his parents. Right after that OHL draft, however, Guelph relocated to Owen

Sound, two hours by car to the J.D. McArthur Arena, which accommodated 4,300.

But Maltby found a home there, quickly establishing himself as a top offensive player willing to mix it up with some physical play. With a six-foot frame that eventually would carry 195 pounds as an NHL skater, Maltby wasn't big as major-junior players went, but he wasn't small either. As a rookie, he scored twelve goals among twenty-seven points, with ninety penalty minutes. By his third season, his NHL draft year, he scored fifty goals and ninety-one points, with ninety-nine PIMs in sixty-four games. Hall of Fame General Manager Glen Sather and legendary scouting director Barry Fraser were impressed enough to spend a third-round pick (sixty-fifth overall) to acquire the prospect for the Edmonton Oilers.

Maltby was accompanied by his parents, brother and a couple of Owen Sound teammates to the 1992 entry draft, held at the Montreal Forum. The days leading up to it were dizzying. His agent had set up a series of interviews with NHL clubs, handed him the itinerary and sent him off. Maltby was on his own, a rather sheltered kid walking around one of his country's largest cities, visiting various hotels to meet with the six or seven clubs that wanted to get to know him a little better. His best interview, he thought, was with Hartford and that's who he expected would draft him. "They seemed to show the most interest," he said. "It went well, but it's kind of funny, I had no idea where Hartford even was."

As it turned out, the Oilers used their second of two third-round picks on Maltby, who would turn out to be, by far, the most successful of the eleven players Edmonton drafted that day. Only four would make it to the NHL. The other three played a total of 124 combined games in the best professional hockey league in the world, most of those games with other teams. Maltby would play 1,072 regular-season NHL games, most of them with Detroit.

The Oilers didn't exactly roll out the red carpet for Maltby, who remembers very little discussion that draft day with anyone on the Oilers staff other than during a chance, casual encounter with Sather. Maltby was with his family, and Sather had noticed that Maltby's brother, Shawn, was wearing an earring. "Glen was busting his chops about that," Kirk said. "That's really about all I remember from that conversation."

Still, it's a memorable day when an NHL club calls your name and claims you as one of its own. Maltby was thrilled. The kid from Hespeler had finally made it. Or had he?

———————

By any reasonable expectation, Kirk Maltby's timing should have been perfect when he showed up for his first NHL training camp in 1992. After one of the most spectacular runs in league history—five Stanley Cup titles in a seven-year span, followed by two more seasons in which the dynastic Oilers advanced to the Western Conference Finals—the club was in desperate need of reinforcements. Most of the top players who had led the Oilers in those Cup runs, guys like Wayne Gretzky, Mark Messier, Jari Kurri, Paul Coffey and many others, were long gone. Edmonton was now in full rebuild mode, starting with four straight seasons of not making the playoffs. How bad was it? Former Red Wing Petr Klima would lead the Oilers in scoring with thirty-two goals and among forty-eight points in the 1992-93 season.

Whether Maltby might have helped as a nineteen-year-old rookie remains a mystery. He didn't get a sniff of an opportunity in his first camp. For reasons he didn't understand and were never explained to him, the Oilers divided their camp into two groups. The vastly larger group included the NHL and other minor pro players and a very few elite youngsters. The other group, Maltby's group, consisted of younger drafted prospects and other training-camp

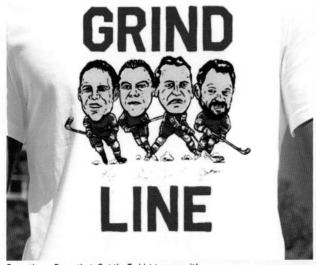

Been there. Done that. Got the T-shirt to prove it!

Kirk Maltby adorns the cover of the nation's leading sports publication in the week ahead of the 1997 Stanley Cup Final. Was he worried about the infamous "SI jinx?" Absolutely he was. But it worked out OK in the end, eh?

Photo courtesy of Roberta McCarty

Craig McCarty and his son, Darren, age about 12, the wannabe Lance Parrish, with plenty of bling to prove he was a pretty good ballplayer, too.

One of the most iconic—and pirated—photos in NHL history. McCarty finally taking care of some long-overdue business with Claude Lemieux, with Brendan Shanahan looking on to make sure McCarty is doing it right. Just behind Shanahan is Colorado defenseman Adam Foote, who's about to get his ass kicked, too. Photo credit to Red Wings team photographer Mark Hicks, who knew immediately he had—perfectly captured a momentous event of March 26, 1997. He alerted the team's merchandising staff, who quickly ordered 100 copies, had them signed and framed them. They sold out within a few hours—at $300 a pop. No Red Wings man cave (or she shed) is complete without one like this.

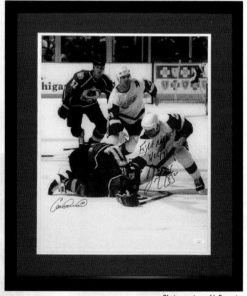

Photo courtesy of I. Dopester

Photo courtesy of John Wharton

Team Halloween parties are legendary across the National Hockey League, and they serve to create some of the most lasting memories. Here, at the Wings' 1996 party, are, from left, Darren McCarty, Kris Draper and Joe Kocur

Photo Courtesy of John Wharton

Kris Draper, right, in an early summer training session when he was well enough to work out after suffering severe facial injuries in Detroit's final playoff game of 1996.

Road warriors—and best friends—Kris Draper and Chris Osgood at pre-playoff paintball outing during a West Coast road trip. It's not all fun and games on the road, but this time it was, with what many teammates described as one of the most galvanizing team events they had ever experienced.

More road warriors: Darren McCarty, Kris Draper and John Wharton behind what looks to be Seal Team Six leader Brendan Shanahan. If you're thinking these guys took this little field trip seriously, you couldn't be more right.

Photo courtesy of John Wharton

Darren McCarty—who else?—driving the bus to the paint-war battle.

Photo courtesy of John Wharton

The winning paint-ball team.

The paint-ball team that finished second.

Everybody loves a winner, eh? Here, actor Mr. T is flanked by John Wharton and Darren McCarty.

On the night before the heartbreaking limo accident, June 12, 1997, John Wharton and Kris Draper had a date with the Stanley Cup.

What is their left to do after returning home from Washington D.C. to celebrate a Stanley Cup championship with the President of the United States? How about meeting up back at The Joe, in the Olympia Room, and opening another case of champagne? Here's McCarty getting drenched. And loving it.

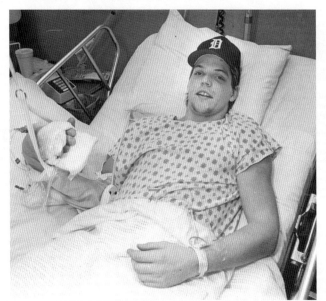

Joe Kocur's NHL career was delayed by several weeks when he nearly lost his right arm to a severe infection following a minor-league fight. After his call-up by the Wings, medics took one look at his injury and rushed him to the hospital, where he underwent emergency surgery to save his limb.

Photo courtesy of John Wharton

Joe Kocur's NHL career ended quite nicely, eh? With two Stanley Cup rings in 1997-98, following the one he earned in 1994 as a member of the New York Rangers. He added a fourth as an assistant to Scotty Bowmen when Detroit won the Cup again in 2002. In this photo, Kocur and John Wharton are on their way from The Joe to Woodward Avenue for the start of the Stanley Cup Parade in 1997.

invitees, a sort of developmental group that got very little development or mentoring in that camp.

"I didn't get in any exhibitions games, and not one practice with
any of the NHL players," he said. "When I look back on it, yeah,
it was disappointing. We got a chance to watch those guys practice, and it would have been nice. I just figured that's how training
camps went ."

After that rather forgettable first NHL camp, Maltby was assigned
to the Oiler's top farm club in Cape Breton, Nova Scotia, 3,100 miles
away on the opposite end of the continent. Yet as bad as Edmonton
was that season, and as well as Maltby and some of his teammates
were playing in Cape Breton, there were very few promotions—and
Maltby wasn't among them. But he thoroughly enjoyed himself in his
first professional season, scoring twenty-two goals among forty-five
points, with 130 penalty minutes to help lead his team to a Calder
Cup championship. Kind of a big deal. He was promoted to the NHL
roster the following fall, but spent the next two seasons in and out of
the lineup in Edmonton. By his third NHL season, 1995-96, it was
increasingly clear that he didn't fit into the Oilers' plans.

Clearly, Kirk Maltby hadn't made it yet, but he was about to be
thrown a lifeline.

———————

Scotty Bowman was sitting across the table at Millie's, a popular restaurant in Sarasota, Florida, run by a Greek family. "The
Greeks, they know restaurants eh?" Bowman was saying on that
gorgeous mid-February morning. More of a statement than a
question. Who's to argue anyway? Just as he was about to describe
the trade, the one he orchestrated that brought Maltby to Detroit,
the waitress arrived to take our order. "Mr. Bowman," a well-
known patron of the diner where everyone from the owner to the
wait staff fawned over him, ordered first, of course.

"Bring me a couple of poached eggs and toast, water with lemon and black coffee," he said. "Put the poached eggs on an English muffin, well done on the muffin. And the eggs, I don't want them runny. Make them medium well."

His voice oozed authority, as if he were describing to his players what he expected them to do on the penalty kill. The day before, he had just returned from a quick round-trip to Pittsburgh, where he was invited to the ceremony honoring Jaromir Jagr on his number retirement. Approaching the age of ninety-one, Bowman showed no sign of slowing down. Still, a gentle prod to bring him back to the subject: the Maltby trade.

Sather, who drafted Maltby into the NHL, once played for Bowman when they were with the Montreal Canadians. Sather was a role player, similar in style to Kris Draper, always played hard, always positive, Bowman said. Now Sather was calling to inquire about a defenseman Detroit had in its prospect pool. Dan McGillis. Detroit had drafted McGillis in the tenth round, 238th overall, out of Northeastern University in 1992—Maltby's draft year. Bowman spoke with Devellano and Holland, and both confirmed that the Wings had little interest in signing McGillis to a pro contract.

"When I called Sather back, he gave me three names (from the Oilers' player list), and Maltby was on the list," Bowman said. Of course he immediately remembered the hit Maltby put on Paul Coffey, so he made a few quick calls to team scouts, doing his due diligence before pulling the trigger on the deal. Maltby had suffered a bad eye injury, which forced him to play with a shield, but other than that there were no issues. Bowman phoned Sather back and made the deal, one for one, McGillis for Maltby.

For those keeping score at home, that's two Grind Liners secured from the 1992 entry draft: McCarty with Detroit's second-round pick and Maltby, acquired in a trade for Detroit's tenth pick that year. At the time, Bowman figured he was making, essentially, a minor league. Which is pretty much what Maltby figured as well when he learned he was traded to Detroit, of all places.

Maltby had just completed the rather complicated journey from Cape Breton, where he had played four games in a conditioning stint after missing time because of an injury. The injury? He took a puck in the right eye after a slapshot by Dallas defenseman Kevin Hatcher. Hence the visor forever after. Just as Maltby, his luggage and his equipment arrived in Pittsburgh, he was greeted by coach Ron Low with the news: "We just traded you to Detroit."

Detroit? That team everyone in hockey believed was on the cusp of a championship season? How lucky can a guy get? Or not.

"To be honest with you, I was devastated," Maltby confessed. "In Edmonton, we weren't going to make the playoffs, but we were a young team, coming up. All I could think of was, *what does Detroit want with me? What am I going to do there?* Everybody in the world, or at least North America, who ever watched a sports channel knew the Red Wings were just crushing everyone. I'm a plumber. A fourth-line guy, and I'm getting traded to this team?"

In newspapers around the continent, the trade would be announced in small, agate type under "Transactions." In the Detroit papers, the trade was covered with a brief note of a few paragraphs at the bottom of Red Wings routine daily beat coverage. To Maltby, however, this was a life-altering earthquake. "I was leaving all I knew, my teammates, the team that drafted me, the city of Edmonton," he said. "I didn't know what was to come afterward."

Seriously, who could have predicted what would come? Maltby's career with Detroit started out with a snowstorm. He was sitting in Pittsburgh with the Wings playing in Toronto that night. Too late for him to get to Toronto in time, and, practically, too soon for the Wings to figure out how and where Maltby might fit in, he flew straight to Detroit. Meantime, the Wings got socked in by the snow and spent an extra day in Ontario.

"So I'm in the Pontchartrain (Hotel) for a day-and-a-half all by myself. I'm a small-town Canadian kid and, I know Detroit is not New York. But it felt like it. All I knew about how to get around was walking from the hotel, through Cobo Hall to Joe Louis Arena."

He was in the Detroit dressing room when his newest teammates finally arrived back from Toronto. In walked Nicklas Lidstrom, followed by Paul Coffey. In came Steve Yzerman and Sergei Fedorov. Maltby had played a bit against the Wings while in Edmonton, but suddenly, he was a bit starstruck. Associate coach Barry Smith introduced Maltby around the room. The only guy on Detroit's roster that Maltby felt like he knew was Darren McCarty, from playing against him in the OHL, and Coffey, from that big hit in Edmonton.

Then Smith took Maltby aside and asked him what seemed like a strange question. "It sort of came out of left field," Maltby said.

"Can you skate backward?" Smith asked. Maltby was confused. *I'm thinking, whoa, what am I getting set up for here? Can I skate backward?*

"Sure I can," Maltby responded, thinking everyone is on the same page.

They weren't. "Next thing I know, I'm on a line with Stu Grimson and Doug Brown. Doug played center, and they put me on right wing. Stu was on the left, and with the system Detroit played—the left-wing lock—the left winger was like a third defenseman."

The unit didn't get a ton of ice time, but eventually Maltby was able to demonstrate his worth as a backward skater. "It was kind of odd. I was coming from a rebuilding team in Edmonton, but as soon as I got to Detroit, the expectations there were so high. They already had the disappointing loss to New Jersey, the upset to San Jose. There were setting all these records, and for me it was like, 'Holy crap!' You could tell their entire focus, they had one goal and one goal only: winning the Stanley Cup. That was my first taste of it at the NHL level. It was a pretty big transition."

To say the Wings were pleased with their new teammate would be an understatement. "He was a tremendous addition for us," Yzerman said. "A really great addition. I remember playing against him. He was fast. He was heavy. He just ran you over. And he was a really good guy, always upbeat, always a smile on his face, always got along with everyone. He was a great teammate, exactly what our team needed at the time."

With Maltby on their roster, the Wings enjoyed the greatest regular season of any team in the history of the NHL. Detroit finished with 131 points, thanks to a league-record sixty-two victories in eighty-two games to win the President's Trophy in a runaway. But their best-laid plans went awry in the conference finals, when they were beaten in six games by Colorado. That season ended with Kris Draper needing surgery and serious dental work after he took that shot from behind by Avalanche forward Claude Lemieux in the final game of the season. It was a game that confirmed Bowman's darkest instincts about his team: his roster was still a work in progress and changes needed to be made if this team was to reach the NHL's summit.

Changes were made, which only heightened the expectations—*and* the ensuing stress and pressure on the team to end its Stanley Cup drought that dragged across more than four decades. Bowman spent the first half of the 1996-97 season tinkering with his lines. He seemed to like playing Kris Draper and Maltby together, especially on the penalty kill. But Maltby wasn't getting sustained playing minutes on any line he could call home. Then, as the holiday season approached, the rumor mill revved up and rocked his world again.

"All of a sudden, we're hearing rumors about signing this Joe Kocur guy," Maltby said, "and I thought, 'well, this is the beginning of the end for me.' I can count. We can only carry so many forwards, and I knew where I stood on the depth chart."

When training camp broke in September, Maltby had been holed up at the Renaissance Center hotel until he was told to find another, more permanent place to live; he had made the final roster as the twelfth or thirteenth forward. "They had a hell of a team, and I was just happy to be there," Maltby said. "Then Bob Probert came in (to JLA) with Chicago and pushed us around. We had some toughness on our team with Shanny (Brendan Shanahan), Marty (Lapointe) and Mac (McCarty). But we needed those guys to play, not sit in the penalty box. But if we bring in Kocur, that's one guy over the roster limit, and now I'm wondering: Who's going to be the odd man out."

It wouldn't be Maltby, though he was anything but secure with his status in the NHL. That would soon change, finally.

"Sometime in the new year (1997) it was me, Drapes and Joey on a line," Maltby said. "It's not like we went out and dominated like the Russian Five. But we played a lot together. . . and it kind of just snowballed."

Toward the end of the season, as the playoffs approached, Bowman continued to tinker with the line, deploying McCarty on the right wing in certain situations, like when the team faced a critical face-off late in a game. For a winger, McCarty was outstanding on the draws, and Bowman liked him out there in case Draper got tossed.

Four guys, one line, still in need of a name, with a lot of work yet to be done at the start of the Stanley Cup playoffs. Before it all ended—and they would have much to say about how it ended—The Grind Line would have its name. And when the Stanley Cup Final started in Philadelphia, they would realize their greatest distinction. But not before more than a little handwringing about a certain, notorious curse.

The week the Stanley Cup Final began, *Sports Illustrated* magazine put the Red Wings on its cover. The image, which screamed more than a thousand words, shows Kirk Maltby front and center, skating away from Eric Messier of the Colorado Avalanche, Detroit's archnemesis in those years. The fierce and brutal rivalry captured the attention of the sporting world across the continent.

"Lucky. Super lucky and honored," Maltby said. "But I also do remember at the time thinking, *it's the cover of S.I. The jinx!* I mean, we hadn't won the Stanley Cup yet. But absolutely cool, yes. And no disrespect to Eric Messier, but you're trying to sell magazines and you've got me and him on the cover of the most famous sports magazine in the country – if not the world? But obviously it was about the crests on the front of our jerseys, and the rivalry."

The reaction from his teammates, on the other hand? "Yeah, they busted my balls for sure," he said. "I've had a lot of various nicknames, good, bad or indifferent, but now all of a sudden they're calling me 'S.I.' Oh my God, give me a break. But that's the beauty of sports, taking ribbings from the guys you loved being around. It could have been a lot worse, and at the end of the day I was honored."

But if Maltby was feeling good about himself and his team with the publication of that *Sports Illustrated* cover, Scotty Bowman was about to take it to a whole new level. And here's where Landon Maltby was about to finally get the answer to his question about when his father finally felt like he'd made it. By May 31, 1997, the date of the first game of the Cup Final, Maltby had played 260 games in the NHL, all but twenty-four in the regular season.

Everybody in hockey knew which line would start for Philadelphia, the so-called Legion of Doom, the biggest line in the NHL if not the best, as many had described it. They were the most fearsome three-man unit in the NHL, bullying their way all the way to Stanley Cup Final, where pundits predicted they would lay waste to the Detroit Red Wings much the same way the New Jersey Devils did two years before in a four-game sweep in the Final.

Bowman's challenge was simple enough: If the Red Wings could stop the Legion of Doom they had an excellent chance to win their first Stanley Cup title in forty-two years. Sure, but how?

When referee Bill McCreary dropped the puck at center ice, there, of course, was the hulking Lindros for the Flyers. And for Detroit, diminutive by comparison, was Kris Draper.

"Scotty put our line, me, Mac and Drapes, out there against the best line in hockey. Holy shit!" Maltby said, describing this thoughts at that moment.

As he wrote in the foreword to this book, Bowman liked starting the Grind Line in important situations like these to set the tone. Which they did spectacularly in Game 1 against the Flyers. And it was that small-town kid from Hespeler Village, the one who constantly battled a kind of imposter syndrome, getting the party started. Now, finally and truly, Maltby could say with more than a little confidence that he belonged.

"Game One of the Stanley Cup Final and I'm there against the Legion of Doom?" he said. "I'm extremely grateful to Scotty for that. I can honestly say that's one of the most honorable things I've ever been given. Or earned."

Earned? Yes, by all means. Earned works.

A Comeback for the Ages

In the dog days of summer 1996 leading up to training camp, John Wharton's phone rang. The Red Wings' athletic therapist was surprised to hear the big boss on the other end of the line. A rather odd time, he thought, but Wharton immediately surmised that Jim Devellano, the team's senior vice president and one third of what was widely known as "the three-headed monster" of a management team, was calling for a welfare check on Kris Draper.

Among Wharton's off-season responsibilities that summer was looking after Draper, whose mug was mangled, facial bones broken and jaw wired shut in that ugly incident during Detroit's final game in Colorado a few months before. But no, Devellano was calling for a very different reason: to inform Wharton that he would be playing golf the following day at the renowned Oakland Hills Country Club. His foursome would include team captain Steve Yzerman, a club member, defenseman Aaron Ward and Joe Kocur. It didn't take long for Wharton—a duffer at best in those days—to figure out this was more of a covert assignment than a casual outing on one of America's premier tracks.

"I was on a spy mission," Wharton recalled.

Although he had been with the Wings for a few years, Wharton had never met Kocur, who made his bones years before in Detroit as the tag-team partner with the renowned Bob Probert. Traded to New York before Wharton's arrival, Kocur's tenure with the Rangers had ended when shipped traded him to Vancouver late in the 1995-96 season. He played seven uneventful games for the Canucks, who inexplicably chose not to re-sign him. By all appearances it seemed like his NHL career was finished. But Kocur was hardly ready to call it a career. He knew he had something left in the tank. And after watching Claude Lemieux cheap-shot Draper in the season finale against Colorado the previous spring, Kocur was sure he knew the team that needed him the most.

Immediately after finding himself jobless, Kocur began lobbying anyone who would listen, pleading for another shot with the Wings. His main subject was Dave Lewis, an assistant to coach Scotty Bowman and Kocur's former teammate with the Wings. To stay in condition, Kocur joined an adult recreation league in at the Lakeland Arena in Waterford Township, Michigan, where the only thing remotely related to hockey for most of the skaters was . . . beer. Win or lose, hockey and hops are inseparable companions. But Kocur also hit the gym.

"I was in the best shape of my life," he said. "I could bench (press) over 400 pounds."

His campaign to get back into the National Hockey League was relentless. "I can still play. I know I can help," was Kocur's mantra when he spoke with Lewis. "Talk to Scotty. Ask him to give me a chance to prove it."

Lewis put him off as long as he could. "I finally said something to Scotty just to get him off my back," said Lewis, who admits to being curious himself about whether Kocur had any game left or any punch to his game.

Kocur also lobbied some of his former Detroit teammates, guys who saw firsthand and were the beneficiaries of his presence both on the ice and in the dressing room. Among them was Yzerman, who clearly was part of the conspiracy setting up the golf outing at Oakland Hills that day. But Kocur didn't stop there. Bowman was getting an earful about the preeminent tough guy at the oddest places.

"I remember stopping at a car dealership after practice," Bowman said. "And Kocur obviously had some friends there, Jerry Vought was one of them, and Bob Moran. And they were all asking me if we were going to sign him."

Wharton accomplished his clandestine mission, as it were. He'd watched Kocur grip it and rip it for a few holes on the golf course, and as they were making small talk getting ready to tee-off on another hole, Wharton casually asked what he'd hoped was a rather innocent question about that notorious, badly scarred right paw.

"So Joey, how's that hand doing?" Wharton inquired.

"Who's asking?" Kocur responded. He'd sniffed it out as soon as he was introduced to Wharton. Why else would an athletic trainer—who couldn't golf—be tagging along with three NHL players in a foursome at a place like Oakland Hills? Kocur knew that Wharton had been sent to check out the hand that constantly worried Devellano, the hand that inflicted so much damage but got Kocur hospitalized more than once in his career. Devellano needed serious assurances before he would even consider agreeing to sign Kocur to another contract in Detroit.

"Well, the truth is," Devellano acknowledged, "when Scotty mentioned he might be interested in signing Joey Kocur, the first thing I asked him was 'What about his hand Scotty? I'm not sure how much more abuse he can take. That hand was a mess."

When the Wings signed Bowman, they gave him a lot of room

to maneuver his roster, especially after his first season behind the bench, when Bryan Murray's tenure as GM had ended. And though the Wings continued to score a lot of goals and pile up victories, Bowman was still uncomfortable with his lineup.

"He didn't like the makeup of our team at all," Devellano said. "He was constantly fighting with Dino Ciccarelli, with Ray Sheppard. And he didn't like Paul Coffey. When we brought Scotty in, the idea was to give him a big say in personnel. I mean, you don't bring in a coach like Scotty Bowman and say, 'Oh, by the way, this is your team. You're going to have to play these guys.' You can do that with other coaches. You don't do that with Scotty Bowman."

Now Bowman was at least mildly interested in rescuing Kocur from the beer-league scrap heap, and Devellano couldn't help but wonder why. "Scotty, what if he can't fight anymore?"

Bowman's response surprised Devellano. "Oh, I don't want him to fight," the coach said. "I think he can help us defensively."

Bowman, who even into his 90s probably watches more hockey than anybody on the planet, had a book on every player he'd ever seen. Catalogued and cross-checked into the deepest recesses of his redoubtable mind. He'd witnessed Kocur becoming a more complete player in New York, especially in the defensive zone where teams win Stanley Cups.

"Joey changed his game," said Dave Lewis. He had to learn how to play better defense, and he did after leaving Detroit. He understood the game better. He became harder to play against. Not just in a physical sense, the fighting, but in his stance. He was hard to get around. Hard to win a battle against. All those little things that Scotty appreciated."

Wharton reported to Devellano that Kocur's hand appeared to be just find. The thick ropes of scars over his knuckles stretching back past the wrist, evidence of the wounds that nearly cost him his career, were receding. He wasn't at all favoring the hand that had inflicted so much abuse on opponents' heads—and helmets. Plus, Kocur was driving the golf ball like a touring pro.

A few phone calls later, Kocur was on his way toward graduating from beer-league hockey in suburban Detroit, to the San Antonio Dragons of the International Hockey League. He played five games there, scoring a goal, assisting on another and racking up twenty-four penalty minutes. More important, he played under the watchful eye of Detroit's pro scout Mark Howe, one of Bowman's most trusted sources.

"He can still play," Howe told Bowman. That was all the coach needed to hear. But Kocur, who had no idea the Wings had sent Howe down to see him, wasn't taking any chances. He knew there was a sure-fire way to convince the Wings that they desperately needed him—a kind of nuclear option—and he wasn't afraid to deploy it. But it wasn't until after that memorable 1996-97 season was finished, after raising the Stanley Cup and the parade celebration, did Joe Kocur finally share his rather sinister scheme to his teammates. And what a confession!

The team had gathered at Mike and Marian Ilitch's Bloomfield Hills estate to celebrate their championship season. Darren McCarty remembers the event for the biggest mountain of cold, succulent shrimp he'd ever seen, and some unforgettable words from his coach. Kris Draper remembers it for the whopper of a confession Kocur finally got off his chest.

"We were sitting there in the backyard, a bunch of us," Draper said, "and Joey took a big breath, he leaned back and said, 'Boys, I've got a little story to tell you.'"

And then they finally understood the astonishing lengths he was willing to take resurrect his NHL career. His plan involved an accomplice—a former teammate then playing for another team—and a borderline treasonous attack on the very team Kocur was hoping to re-join.

His plan began to unfold on October 25, 1996, when the Chicago Blackhawks made their first of three visits that season to Joe Louis Arena. Eight days earlier, the Wings lost a spirited 2-1 decision in Chicago—Slava Fetisov scoring the lone Detroit goal on assists from Vladimir Konstantinov and Draper. As it happens among traditional archrivals, the temperatures rose for the prickly rematch in Detroit. Chicago was its usual ornery aggressive self, taking advantage of the fact that earlier in the month, the Wings lost their heavyweight enforcer, Stu Grimson, on waivers. Former Wings tough guy Bob Probert set the tone with a couple of roughing penalties in the first period, which featured fifty penalty minutes, thirty-one to Chicago. The game ended in a 2-2 overtime draw, Slava Kozlov and Brendan Shanahan scoring for Detroit. There were a total of eighty-four penalty minutes in the match, which played directly into Kocur's hands. He attended the game for the expressed purpose of having a private chat with his pal Probert. But he made it a point to be seen by the Detroit contingent.

"I remember running into Mr. Ilitch before the game in the lot where the players parked," Kocur said. "He came over to say hi. He stuck his hand in the window, grabbed my arm, and said, 'Holy shit. We've got to get you back!'"

Draper remembers seeing Kocur after the game. "He had on this white T-shirt, and I just saw the size of his arms, his back, and more importantly, his hands," he said. "And I'm thinking, 'Oh. My. God.'"

Kocur was ripped like one of the stars on the professional wrestling circuit, minus the glistening oil—6-feet, 223 pounds of chiseled granite. Every farm-bred muscle made an impression beneath that shirt. Anyone who saw him couldn't help but wonder: "Can this guy still play?" And answer immediately: "He sure as hell looks like it."

So that part of his mission was accomplished. The more important element to his plan involved a visit to the Chicago dressing room to see his buddy. And as soon Probert showered and dressed, Kocur pulled him aside.

"Look, the next time you guys come to play here, you've got to do something. Start some shit. Make Detroit realize they need to get tougher. Just come in here and do something crazy."

Probert smiled, as though nothing would make him happier. True to his word—because nothing made Bob Probert happier than being Bob Probert—when the Hawks returned to the Joe on December 12, he brought the carnage. And some of his worst-mannered teammates came along for the ride.

"Before we took the ice, I told the boys, 'Come on guys. Let's get out there and kick the crap out of them,'" Probert said in his book, "The Bruise Brothers," written with Kocur and Windsor sports writer Bob Duff. "And we did."

Less than two minutes into the game, Probert ran goaltender Mike Vernon, then fought Brendan Shanahan, igniting a line brawl. With less than five minutes remaining in the period, he fought Darren McCarty. And in the third period, Bob Probert simply snapped.

"He just went cuckoo," Kocur said in his portion of the book. At the 6:25 mark, young Wings defenseman Jamie Pushor stepped up to try his luck against Probert. He got knocked out. Probert was slapped with three majors—attempt to injure, misconduct, and game misconduct. His night was over with more than thirteen minutes left to play in the game, but he tallied forty-nine of Chicago's sixty-nine penalty minutes in the game—and the entire Red Wings team had a front-row seat to all of it.

"It was all right there in our end," Draper said, "and it was pretty obvious. We just didn't have an answer for the Chicago Blackhawks." No answer, in particular, for Mr. Probert.

The Wings won that game, overcoming a 2-0 first-period deficit with six unanswered goals. Steve Yzerman, Sergei Fedorov and Brendan Shanahan each had a goal and an assist. But anyone who saw that game knew, in no uncertain terms: Stanley Cup dreams be damned, the Detroit Red Wings were vulnerable.

The one guy who didn't witness the carnage was Joe Kocur, who by then was getting his legs back with that minor-league stint in San Antonio. And not long after that, he was home in Highland Township for the holiday break when his phone rang. It was the evening of December 23.

"Joe Kocur? Scott Bowman. Have your team send your stuff back here. We're signing you."

Merry Christmas. Featuring Scotty Bowman as Kris Kringle. And Bob Probert as Elf.

Suffice to say that Draper and his teammates were astounded to hear the rest of that story, how Kocur orchestrated his return to the NHL. He had turned the greatest enforcer, the most feared fighter in the league against them for a single night of mayhem in their own building. But it worked.

"Guys, I needed a job," Kocur told his teammates. Then they had another beer.

"Sure enough, that game led to Joey signing with us," Draper said, laughing again as he recounted the moment. "Obviously, one of the greatest stories you could ever hear."

And it gets better.

"Next thing I knew," Probert said in his book, "Joe was back in the NHL with Detroit, and there he was, lined up opposite me for a face-off in a game at the United Center."

Yep the second game after his return to the NHL, Kocur and the Wings traveled to Chicago for another match with the Blackhawks. And the drama continued to unfold. Barely two minutes into the game, Pushor and Hawks pugilist Jim Cummins went off for fighting. On the ensuing face-off, Bowman sent Kocur out for his third shift, and he found himself standing next to Probert. Kocur greeted his pal with his stick, whacking him across the shins. In hockey parlance, that an invitation to dance.

"Probie, we've got to go," Kocur said.

"Oh yeah, sure," Probert said, dismissing the notion.

"No, Probie. Let's go."

"C'mon, man," Probert countered. "I helped you get back in the game."

The puck dropped and the gloves came off. The pair Wings fans so lovingly embraced as the Bruise Brothers, *their* Bruise Brothers, began exchanging haymakers.

"That wasn't for show either," Kocur said. "We really were trying to beat each other up."

And the crowd, of course, went wild. One of Kocur's favorite pictures from his entire career is of that fight, with fans in the background going crazy. Eventually, the combatants fell to the ice.

"I just remember looking at him and saying, 'Probie, I love you. Thanks for getting me back in the league."

"No problem, man," Probert said as he skated toward the penalty box. Truth be told, however, Probert was confused—and a little bit ticked off. He felt he had been duped, betrayed by his good pal. And it wasn't until years later, when he and Kocur wrote their book together, that Kocur explained the importance of his proving his value to the team that just brought him back into the league. Probert understood that and he accepted it.

"You know, he won three Stanley Cups after his return to Detroit," Probert said. "He still thanks me for that."

That tussle in Chicago was actually the second time the Bruise Brothers exchanged punches. They went at it the first time in 1993, when Kocur was with the New York Rangers and Probert in his last days in Detroit.

"He whacked me in the side of the head," Probert said. "Thank God he didn't hit me square, because I didn't see it coming until the last second. He hit me in the helmet, but he still rocked me. Neither bout was a big issue with us. We were just doing our jobs. The next time we saw each other, we laughed about it."

Gregory Joseph Kocur (the internet is wrong; his name is not Joseph George Kocur, like Google thinks) was born four days before Christmas in 1964, the only son of Joe and Rita Kocur on a mile-square— that's 640 acres—grain farm in Kelvington, Saskatchewan. It's a tiny prairie town that grows big-time hockey players as well as it does wheat, oats, corn, canola and barley, among other crops.

Nobody called him Greg or Gregory. He's a third-generation Joe in the Kocur clan, so quite naturally he grew up being called Joey. That worked fine for him as a kid, but as an adult he prefers to be called Joe. A man's name, right? That's his thinking, at any rate. But to family, friends and fans, he'll always be Joey. Their thinking: he's just not a regular Joe, and that "y" on the end carries a mountain of affection. Besides, even as he approached his sixties, Kocur still flashed a cherubic smile that lights up the room, like the eight-year-old who just scored the winning goal.

Kelvington sits at the intersection of Highway 38 and Highway 49, about a three-hour drive east of Saskatoon. Anyone rolling into town from the south end will realize this is serious hockey country. On the west side of Highway 38 are four, four-foot-by-eight-foot banners—actually oversized hockey cards created by local artist Edd Feairs—announcing this as the birthplace of some highly recognizable National Hockey League stars: four-time Stanley Cup champion Joey Kocur; his cousin, Kory Kocur, the former first-round pick (seventeenth overall in 1988) of the Detroit Red Wings; former Red Wing player, serial-winning coach and pre-eminent broadcaster Barry Melrose; and, perhaps the most famous of all, at least in Canada, Wendel Clark, the first-overall draft pick and long-time captain of the Toronto Maple Leafs who had a cup of coffee in Detroit near the end of his career.

The Kocurs and Melrose are cousins through marriage. But in his book, Kocur clarifies one longtime and widespread misconception: he and Wendel are not cousins. Close, like family, but not family. Neighbors, too, and by that we're talking a three-mile walk from the Kocur homestead to the Clarks' place.

Related or not, the Clarks were good people to know. Not only were there three boys to hang around with—Donn, the best man at Joe Kocur's wedding, Wendel and Kerry—but their dad, Les, ran the ice arena in Kelvington. It was conveniently located just a few steps, literally, from the town schoolhouse.

"The front door of the rink was right opposite the back door of the high school," Kocur said in his book. "At the old rinks, they'd shovel the snow from the ice machine and pile it up outside. We'd come running from the school on our lunch hour and dive through this little pathway—about two feet by two feet—between the piles of snow. Once inside, we'd run across the ice to get our gear on and skate."

But hockey wasn't their only sporting passion. In those glorious summers on the prairie fastball fueled their passion. The Clark and Kocur boys, along with Melrose and Kelly Chase from nearby Porcupine Plain, formed the nucleus of strong, athletic team that could compete with Canada's best. Kocur played second or third base, sometimes left field. Wendel Clark had the speed to cover a lot of ground in centerfield. Melrose, big and slow on the diamond or the ice, played first base. Chase could play anywhere in the infield or outfield.

Kocur remembers batting against Gene McWillie, who won a gold medal at the 1983 Pan-American Games and annually led Canada to the International Softball Congress championship tournament. McWillie had a pitch—underhanded, windmill-style—clocked at eight-seven miles per hour. "Like trying to hit a shot put," is how Kocur described it. Both Kocur and Clark went on to play semi-pro fastball for the Rempel Brothers in Saskatoon for a few seasons until hockey overtook their lives.

Meanwhile, life on a working family farm was anything but fun and games. Saskatchewan is a global leader in agriculture, producing more than a third of the world's total exported durum wheat. It's also the top exporter of lentils and dry peas. And all that production is the result of a lot of hard work. It's why so many National Hockey League general managers and scouts are partial to prospects from Western Canada: they're raised with an incomparable work ethic.

"I really like the Western Hockey League," said Devellano, who drafted several of them when he was helping to build the New York Islanders dynasty of the early 1980s. "Those were big, strong farm boys who already knew the value of hard work. And they were well-prepared for the NHL, traveling coast to coast on those fucking iron lungs (buses). They wanted to be hockey players."

For Saskatoon, Kocur's junior team in the WHL, the closest bus trip was provincial rival Regina, two hours away. "After that, our closest trip was Winnipeg (Manitoba), ten hours away. Some trips, we'd be on the bus for twenty-four hours straight."

Small price to pay for some of them because it was the fastest and surest way to get the hell off the farm where everyone works even longer, harder hours year round.

"Every day was a work day," Kocur recalled. While his sisters, Lisa and Lana, stayed around the house to help their mother, cooking, cleaning, and tending the gardens that helped to feed their family, Joey would get home from school, grab a quick bite to eat and get to wherever his father was, prepared to help with whatever was needed at the time. Pick stones, tote bales of hay, "all of that crap," is how he described it. Of all his myriad duties, Kocur figures he spent more hours picking rocks and stones out of the headland and tossing them into the tree line. The headland is the twenty or thirty yards of land on the edges of a planted field, known more commonly in the United States as the turnrow. Picking stones, rocks and boulders and carrying them to the trees. "That would be my whole day," Kocur explained, a tone of disdain in his voice.

Like so many Canadian boys in that era, Kocur found himself on skates not long after he learned to walk, skating on the nearby sloughs that froze over. He soon discovered he was pretty good at hockey—and it was a lot more fun than working the farm. He seemed to always lead his league in scoring, sometimes by a wide margin. But his career really took off when he joined Yorkton, of the Tier II Saskatchewan Junior Hockey League. He was fourteen, playing both Midget hockey and for the senior men's team, the Kelvington Wheat Kings in the Fishing Lake Hockey League. Double the ice time, double the pleasure. Didn't matter that he was a slender 160 pounds playing against men as old as forty-five and weighing as much as 250 pounds. He was having a blast.

Kocur made the team in Yorkton on his second try, and there, under the tutelage of renowned coach Gerry James, is where a good young hockey player was transformed into a great future NHL prospect. Kocur's eyes glow when he speaks of James, who as an enforcer-type winger played parts of five seasons with the Toronto Maple Leafs and twelve seasons as a running back for the Canadian Football League's Winnipeg Blue Bombers and the Saskatchewan Roughriders. In fact, James played in the Stanley Cup Final vs. Montreal in 1960, just a few months after kicking a field goal and converting two touchdowns in Winnipeg's 1959 Grey Cup win over Hamilton.

James was an all-business, no-nonsense coach, too, commanding the respect of everyone in his lockerrooms. Two months into his first season in Yorkton, Kocur was still trying to find himself, unsure of how or where he fit on his team. That's when he was summoned to James' office for a conversation that changed his life. Actually, it was more of a monologue. James spoke. Kocur listened. He listened carefully.

"If you want to go anywhere in this sport, then you've got to do something better than anyone else," the coach said. "You've got to find your niche, whether it's goal scorer, passer, whatever you do, you've got to be the best at it."

Then James started talking about physical play, planting a seed. To this day, Kocur can't really say if it was James who convinced him to develop his enforcer skills, but it wasn't long before Kocur started playing tougher, fighting more, enjoying it—and finding himself. People ask him all the time how or when it was that he became a fighter. This was when. And how he got good at it was simply a matter of practice. A lot of practice. That first year with the Yorkton Terriers of the Saskatchewan Junior Hockey League, Kocur logged 307 minutes in the penalty box while scoring six goals among fifteen points in just forty-eight games.

"At some point, I had gotten into a couple of fights and thought, 'Well, this isn't too bad,'" Kocur said. "So I ended up getting into a lot of fights that year."

The transition from star offensive player to feared enforcer was fairly smooth—for him. For his parents, not so much. "I don't know that it bothered Dad that much," he said, "but Mum would sit in the stands and put her hands over her eyes—at least until she saw I was getting OK at it. She still had some anxieties, but she wasn't as worried anymore."

With the extra room he created for himself, Kocur improved his offensive skills while fighting less. He ended the season with twenty goals among forty-one points, with 199 penalty minutes in forty-seven games. His graduation to Major Junior Hockey with the Saskatoon Blades of the Western Hockey League seemed effortless.

"In Saskatoon, I was still one of the skilled players," he said, "but I was also still getting a lot of penalty minutes." It was his physical game, he said, that gained him notoriety. One fight in particular, in Kamloops, British Columbia, put him on every scout's map.

"They had this coach, Bill LaForge, just a whack job," Kocur said of one of the more entertaining junior coaches of the time. LaForge had a controversial reputation, his teams known for their intimidation tactics, on-ice brawls, suspensions and fines. Joe Kocur was having none of that. "I grabbed one of his kids and knocked him out cold. "That, quite frankly, is one of the biggest reasons I got noticed."

Certainly, Wayne Meier noticed. Meier was a Detroit scout who covered Western Canada—one of Devellano's first hires when he assembled his inaugural scouting staff. Meier had been with the Portland Winter Hawks for ten seasons as a scout and director of player personnel. He knew the territory well, and he put his fingerprints on that first Red Wings draft of the Ilitch ownership era.

The 1983 NHL Entry Draft marked a turning point in Detroit, away from the so-called (and accurate) Dead Wings era. It began with Steve Yzerman, the fourth overall pick, and continued with Lane Lambert, Kocur's Saskatoon Blades teammate, taken in the second round with the twenty-fifth overall pick. Then the Wings headed east to the Ontario Hockey League to take Probert in the third round, forty-sixth overall. The Wings whiffed on their fourth-round pick, but selected two more NHL players in the fifth round—winger Petr Klima out of Czechoslovakia at eighty-six and Kocur two picks later. That's five NHL regulars in the first five rounds who logged a combined total of 4,339 NHL games, a remarkable haul. Most GMs would be happy to draft even two players who can get 400 games each in the NHL.

But the Wings weren't done yet with that 1983 draft. In the tenth round, they snagged Stu Grimson, another WHL enforcer out of Regina. The third significant Meier draftee that year.

"Detroit was going tough," Kocur said in his book, adding that if the Wings were "seeking out weapons of mass destruction. . . (they) certainly found them that day."

Probert ended his career fifth overall in National Hockey League history in penalty minutes, with 3,300 in 935 games. Kocur ranks twenty-first overall, with 2,519 PIMs in 821 games. And Grimson ranks forty-fourth with 2,113 minutes in 729 games. Three of the most-penalized players in league history in a single draft—by one team!

While many teen-aged prospects attended the draft on June 8, 1983, dreaming of hearing their names called by an NHL club, Kocur stayed home and went to work, driving a delivery truck for Reliance Lumber in Kelvington. He suffered no illusions of grandeur.

"At that point in my life, I wasn't thinking about a career in pro hockey," he said, "so it didn't matter to me. I didn't expect to be drafted."

So he was more than a bit surprised when he returned from a lumber-delivery run and was summoned to the office. He had received a phone call. "OK, who from?" Kocur responded. He dialed the return number and learned at that moment that he had been drafted by the Detroit Red Wings. To this day, he cannot recall who he had spoken with on the Detroit end. Could have been Devellano; more likely it was Wayne Meier. Even then, Kocur had a hard time taking it seriously.

"I don't think I ever believed I was going to make it," he said. "Even after I was drafted, I hardly thought about the NHL."

Then he went to his first training camp with the Wings, and, as they also say in hockey, shit got serious.

The big farm kid from Kelvington bullied his way around the ice, hitting without discretion, punching out anyone who wanted a go. He ran star center Danny Gare from behind and knocked him out. He fought defenseman Larry Trader, who needed many stitches to close head wounds. "It was like someone told me to go out and get noticed," Kocur recalled. "And the only way a tough guy can get noticed is by being tough."

He got noticed alright; soon, he had a target on his back. Dave (Tiger) Williams, Detroit's resident brawler—and incidentally the NHL's all-time penalty minute record-holder with 3,971—came after Kocur with his stick. Williams and goaltender Greg Stefan both tried to chop the kid down behind the net. This was when the team was practicing drills. The actual red-white training camp games between teammates were borderline sadistic, Kocur recalled. But those same teammates who wanted to kill him in practice were more than happy to have him along when they played actual NHL opponents in exhibition games. Kocur knew then that he belonged, that he could hang with men in the NHL.

But he wasn't quite ready for prime time yet, the Wings decided. While Yzerman and Lambert easily made a Detroit's talent-starved roster in the fall of 1983, Kocur, like Probert, was returned to his junior team. (Klima wouldn't surface until the summer of 1985, when the Wings orchestrated his dramatic defection while the Czech national team was in West Germany.)

Flush with confidence, Kocur returned to Saskatoon and had a highly productive season. He was one of four forty-goal scorers (forty goals, eighty-one points with 258 penalty minutes in sixty-nine games), but his team failed to make the playoffs. His season wasn't over, however. He got called up to Adirondack, which was playing Maine in an American Hockey League playoff series. Kocur was astonished to find himself on a starting line with a couple of other rugged forwards. Some coaches call them "energy lines." But clearly, as the visiting coach, Bill Dineen wanted to set a certain tone, and Kocur didn't need an Ouija Board to know what kind of tone that might be.

Perhaps because he so amped up playing in his first professional league game. Maybe he just didn't care. In retrospect, Kocur couldn't say. But as he describes his first shift, he was probably about five feet behind a defenseman, who was racing into his own end to touch the puck for an icing call. The whistle blew. But Kocur didn't slow down. "I ran him through the end boards as hard as I possibly could," Kocur said. Got a boarding penalty to start the game. His coach didn't say a word. The tone was set. "I knew why I was out there for the opening face-off. They didn't start me to score a goal."

He continued to make a favorable impression on Detroit's powers that be in his first full professional season, 1984-85, with Adirondack. While chipping in his share of points—twelve goals and nineteen points in forty-seven games—he was piling up penalty minutes (171) and terrorizing opponents. In December of that season, Adirondack was in Halifax, Edmonton's top farm club, when Kocur tangled with another heavyweight destined for the NHL, Jim Playfair. Kocur tagged him in the mouth hard enough to knock out his opponent. In the process, what was left of Playfair's tooth tore a gash on the back of Kocur's right hand.

Moments later, the two were side-by-side in the trainer's room. While medics were working to restore Playfair to functional consciousness, others were sewing up Kocur's hand. It needed twenty stitches. A bit later, coach Bill Dineen informed Kocur that he and goaltender Eddie Mio were getting called up to Detroit. On the trip to Michigan, with a stop at Mama Mio's in Windsor for dinner, Kocur noticed that his hand was starting to swell up. The next morning, at the game-day skate before a match later against Washington, Kocur went to trainer Jim Pengelly to report that his hand was feeling unusually warm.

"I didn't know what was wrong, and I didn't care," Kocur recalled. "I was going to play in the NHL."

No, as it turned out, he wasn't. His hand had ballooned so much that he couldn't slip a glove over his hand. After practice, Kocur showed the trainer his hand, and Pengelly immediately summoned Dr. John Finley, the team physician who took one look at it and sent him directly to the hospital for emergency surgery.

"I'm sure a lot of guys would give their right arm to play in the NHL," Kocur has often joked since then. "But you know what? I almost did."

Hitting Playfair's tooth, doctors later explained, had caused a deep cut in one of his knuckles and the wound got infected after it was sewn up. The surgery, by Dr. Richard M. Singer at Harper-Grace Hospital, started at the knuckle and went at least six inches up Kocur's right arm. "It was all rotting, and they had to clean it up," Kocur said, adding that doctors later told him that if he had gone another six hours without medical attention they would have had to amputate his right arm. He spent two weeks in the hospital, on a morphine drip, the wound on his hand wide open and slowly healing. His NHL career was on hold, but he dodged a bullet that could have ended it all before it ever really began.

When he was fit to play again, Kocur was returned to the minors to get back in shape. In mid-February, he was recalled to Detroit when Tiger Williams was placed on waivers and claimed by the Los Angeles Kings. Kocur finally made his NHL debut on February 20, 1985, in a 3-2 win over St. Louis at Joe Louis Arena. Three days later, he fought his first big-league bout against Jeff Brubaker in a 4-2 loss to Toronto. A few days later, while the Wings were in Philadelphia, the Wings told Kocur they were sending him to Adirondack—to get his stuff and return to Detroit immediately. He was in the NHL to stay.

When he showed up in Glens Falls, however, Kocur had two black eyes, courtesy of fight the night before with the Flyers' Dave Richter. He didn't know Richter was a lefty and took several shots to the mug before he could get the match under control.

Kocur's first full season in the NHL, 1985-86, was memorable in myriad ways. It started with such promise after owner Mike Ilitch went on a spending spree and signed five free-agent college players (including Adam Oates), three touted NHL veterans, and Petr Klima, after orchestrating his defection. They also had a new coach, the affable Harry Neale, who succeeded Nick Polano.

What ensued was "dramady" of epic proportions: Drama that at times made the Wings the laughingstock of the league and embarrassed their ownership and comedy that would make the Keystone Kops proud. Neale was fired over the holiday break that season, replaced by Brad Park, and it got worse. Laughingly, heartbreakingly worse. A *Sports Illustrated* feature, in which the magazine boldly predicted a Stanley Cup for Detroit that season after a visit to the team's training camp in Port Huron, was distant, infuriating memory.

The Wings finished twenty-first in a twenty-one-team league, and it wasn't close. The 1985-86 season remains the worst in the club's nearly century-old existence. But fans showed up in remarkable numbers, and Ilitch didn't even have to give away cars, like he did at every home game a few seasons earlier. No, they were at The Joe—a perfectly named arena for that chapter in Detroit's hockey history—to see Kocur and Probert. The fans came for the fights.

Sure, that was somewhat embarrassing to the club's management. But when the team averaged nearly 18,000 fans per game, and they were gorging themselves on beer and Little Caesars pizza, there wasn't much to complain about. Only the quality of hockey.

"I never thought I'd be the reason that people bought tickets for a game," Kocur said. But he certainly understood the reality. "Give the people what they want," he often said. And, while slogging through lopsided loss after lopsided loss, through the line-brawls and bench-clearing melees, that's what he and Probert did.

Kocur set several club penalty-minute records that season, including 377 he compiled in the sin-bin through fifty-nine games. He also scored nine goals among fifteen points. Probert had 186 penalty minutes, with eight goals among twenty-one points in forty-four games. Soon, "Bruise Brothers" T-shirts were seen all around Detroit and the team's popularity soared after Park was replaced by Jacques Demers. In Demers' first two seasons, incredibly, the Wings went from the NHL's doormat to making the final four of the Stanley Cup tournament, losing each time to the dynastic Edmonton Oilers and Wayne Gretzky in the Western Conference Final.

Kocur's team record for PIMs in a season would last just two years, until Probert amassed 398 (with twenty-nine goals) in a campaign that featured an appearance in the NHL All-Star Game in St. Louis. Probert assisted on a goal by Gretzky in that game.

Life was good for the Red Wings in those years, at least compared to the previous two decades. They were playing barely .500 hockey, but making the playoffs; that was possible when sixteen of the NHL's twenty-one teams advanced to the post-season. While the young captain Steve Yzerman was emerging as one of the league's star offensive players, he had precious little support around him. The Wings won on many nights on the strength of whatever offense Yzerman could provide and their team toughness. Specifically, the

Probert and Kocur show. But while Probert had found a home on Yzerman's wing, Kocur remained a fourth-line role player, whose role was very specific. Still, heady times for both.

Colin Campbell was an assistant to Demers before leaving Detroit and ultimately becoming a top lieutenant of Commissioner Gary Bettman. Campbell often said that it felt like the Wings started every home game with a 1-0 lead, "because the opposing players would be shaking in their boots just jumping over the boards." They were scared. It's hard to play hockey when you're looking over your shoulder all the time. The Wings still weren't very good, but they were the most intimidating team in hockey. Which explains why their fans were walking a little taller, talking a little bolder, and having a lot more fun in those days.

But playoff success was short-lived. The dearth of talent caught up with the Wings, and after four seasons Demers was fired and replaced by Bryan Murray in 1990. Murray also assumed the duties of general manager, with Devellano booted upstairs.

Kocur didn't survive his first season under Murray. In a trade that shocked Detroit's fan base, Murray sent Kocur to the New York Rangers for journeyman center Kevin Miller and two goons, Jim Cummins and Dennis (Mongo) Vial. Kocur was devastated, not only that he was traded but because it was accompanied by a whispering campaign that Kocur didn't want to fight anymore. And if he wouldn't fight, he was of little use.

"That hurt, because I had done everything for the Red Wings, right from the moment I was drafted," said Kocur, who reacted as most of us would when get our hearts broken. He wept.

In retrospect, those rumors that Kocur wasn't interested in performing his role any more were outrageous—and so tragically wrong. He was one of the most active enforcers in the league that season, accumulating 253 penalty minutes in fifty-two games. In one of those fights, on December 1, 1990, with Buffalo tough guy Rob Ray, Kocur suffered a deep tear over the knuckle of his middle finger. As he explains it, over the knuckle bone itself, there is a tendon and a capsule over the tendon, which is covered by the skin. Kocur had torn both the skin, the capsule and split the tendon down the middle, so every time he threw a punch with that hand, he was connecting with exposed bone.

"I couldn't do it anymore it hurt so bad," he said. It was while he was sidelined for three weeks, trying to give the hand some time to heal, that he was traded away—on March 5, 1991. It was a difficult time for him. Not only was he vanquished, but the malicious whispers out of Detroit's front office were damaging his reputation. Fortunately, Kocur had strong supporters in New York. Rangers General Manager Neil Smith had been Detroit's chief scout and an assistant to Devellano during Kocur's formative years with the Wings. And Campbell was then an assistant coach with the Rangers. They immediately recognized that Kocur's hand required serious medical attention. On May 10, he underwent surgery—the tendons spliced together, the capsules put back in place. Another scar, but by training camp the following fall, the hand was fine. No more injury. No more pain. Kocur could fight again, or perform as needed for his new team.

As dark as those early days with the Rangers were, in retrospect Kocur looks back at them rather fondly. Going to the Rangers not only gave him an opportunity to improve and round out his game, but he won a Stanley Cup with them in 1994, which ended 54 years of futility for the franchise.

"If I hadn't won a Cup with the Rangers, I might have said (the trade) was the worst thing that ever happened to me," Kocur said. Arguably, that worst moment came two years after winning, when he was cut loose by the Vancouver Canucks. So began his

unrelenting campaign to prolong his NHL career—with the team
that brought him into the league.

As much as his reputation preceded him, there were some mixed
feelings among some of his new Detroit teammates when Kocur
started practicing with the Wings. Draper was especially curious after Bowman put the tough guy on the other wing with him
and Maltby.

"I'm thinking, 'We're getting Joe Kocur. He's going to be my
right winger. He's been playing in a beer league, and now I'm playing with him in the National Hockey League?'"

Then, a revelation. "Joey was there on the right, and it was
pretty obvious: He's got good hands. Underrated hands. Real skill,"
Draper continued. "All of a sudden, we started having some chemistry. We're cycling pucks. He's holding onto it. And then there's the
intimidation factor around the league for what he does. Malts and
I start seeing we have a little bit more room."

Maltby immediately saw so much more than a brawler in his
new linemate. "People ask me all the time about Joey, how tough he
was. Everybody likes to talk about that, but personally, I don't think
Joey gets near enough accolades for how good a hockey player he
was. Trust me, he was super tough, and there's no question about
that. Shake his right hand and you'll see. But Joey was a hell of a
hockey player, too."

He brought more than better-than-expected skills to team as
well, Maltby added.

"We had a lot of guys who had been to the finals against New
Jersey (in 1995), but there's something different when you go to the
finals and win the Stanley Cup," Maltby said. "The knowledge,
the experience you get from that—I don't know if I ever saw Joe

panicked or nervous, whether he was squaring up to fight a big guy or just going out and playing a regular shift. He was just cool, calm and collected. He always told us, 'Just play your game.' We knew that when we got onto the ice with him that we were going to be just fine."

So Kocur's addition was more than completing another serviceable new forward line. It had a positive ripple effect up and down the Detroit lineup, Yzerman said. "He was given a role that involved more than just go out and fight. He was on a very good line. Now he could just go out and play."

Kocur obviously helped to transform a smaller club that, however talented, was manhandled by New Jersey in the Devils' sweep of Detroit in the 1995 Stanley Cup Final. "Now we were a much bigger team," Yzerman said. "With Malts, who was a pretty heavy guy, and Joey, Marty Lapointe and Brendan Shanahan, just about every line had a 220-pounder, at least one. When Joey came back, it really helped balance our team."

To maintain that balance, though, would require him to change his habits, and Bowman made that clear in a meeting with Kocur as soon as he arrived.

"He called me into his office the first or second morning I was there," Kocur said. "He welcomed me to Detroit and said, 'First things first: I don't want you to fight.' And I'm thinking, 'That's kind of weird. I thought you brought me here for that.'"

And then Bowman explained his thinking.

"If you're sitting in the penalty box, you're not available when I might need you," the coach said. Just as Bowman turned creating uncertainty among his players into an art form, never letting them get comfortable, so he sought to create uncertainty for opponents. If Kocur is on the bench, Bowman has a loaded weapon he can discharge at any time. Meantime, Kocur could just go out and, for the first time in his career, just play hockey.

"It gave me a chance to not worry about every shift having to fight somebody," Kocur said. "I could play with a bit more freedom."

Still, there were times when Kocur did get an itch he needed to scratch. Then he'd sidle up to Draper and whisper in his ear.

"Drapes, I need one tonight. You gotta take a run at this guy, or that guy, get something started," Draper recalled. "And I'd say, 'Joey, I'm a lot faster than you. If I start something, I need you in there quick. And he'd say, 'Just remember, I'm always fast enough.'"

On one of the first of those "itches," Draper recalled, the Wings were in Arizona, where Rick Tocchet was on the loose and trying to make life miserable for Detroit.

"So I took a run at Tocchet," Draper said. "I hit him, caught him pretty good. Then I purposely stumbled a bit and went down. As I got up, all I saw was red gloves come flying off, and it's Joey. He and Tocchet had a helluva fight, and it was a momentum changer for us. And as Joey skated off to the penalty box, all I could think of was, 'Sonofabitch, he is fast enough.'"

Fast forward one last time to the eve of the Stanley Cup Final, 1997.

The Red Wings had survived three grueling playoff rounds. Though they were shut out twice in the opening round against St. Louis, the Wings won the series four games to two. The Grind Line led the way offensively with four goals and four assists in the series. In perhaps the longest, most difficult sweep in NHL playoff history, Detroit dispatched the Anaheim Mighty Ducks, though it needed five overtime periods. The Russian Five dominated the scoring for Detroit, including a goal by Slava Kozlov in triple over-time in Game 2 at The Joe. The Western Conference Final was a battle royale between newly minted archrivals Detroit and Colorado. Each team won a game by the score of 6-0. The Grind Line contributed three goals among five points as Detroit outlasted the Avs, four games to two.

As the Wings were celebrating that series victory over Colorado and a return to the Stanley Cup Final, Kocur—one of two Stanley Cup champions in the room (with defenseman Larry Murphy) came up from behind and whispered into the ear of assistant coach Lewis.

"Guess what?" Kocur whispered. "It gets better."

And he was right.

Bringing the Pugilism

In his forty-two seasons with the Detroit Red Wings, which made him the longest-serving employee in the history of the nearly century-old franchise, Jim Devellano has seen it all. Or at least most of it. The first hire Marian and Mike Ilitch made when they bought the club in 1982, Devellano served as the club's senior vice president, alternate governor and confidante to the two most important people in the organization—Marian and General Manager Steve Yzerman —as the calendar roared toward 2025. And to Devellano's credit, his take on how Scotty Bowman built and coached the Grind Line is beyond fascinating.

While serving as a mentor to Ken Holland in his early years as general manager, and as a trusted adviser to the club owners, Devellano was levels removed from the day-to-day proceedings in his team's lockerroom. But he had eyes and ears everywhere throughout the organization through a network of informants. So when he shared anything related to the inner workings of the team or the business side of the franchise, he had a certain built-in credibility. That, combined with the fact that lying made him more than uncomfortable, made him a fairly trusted and reliable source of information.

So when Jim Devellano explained during an interview in his elegant retirement community in Sarasota, Florida in February 2024 how Bowman managed the Grind Line, we could take that to the bank, right? Well, perhaps not, as it turns out.

"Here's the beauty of Scotty Bowman," Devellano began. "He would call them in—they were all a little scared of him, and when he called them in it wasn't to be friendly—he was going to deliver a message that went like this: 'You guys have got one fucking job to do and that's to keep the fucking puck out of our net. When you guys are on the ice, we don't get scored on. Period. You're going to get twelve fucking minutes a game. You're here to give Yzerman, Fedorov and their lines a breather. And I'm not putting any pressure on you to score, but don't you fucking dare get scored on.'

"Well, that took all the pressure off them," Devellano continued, "because now all they had to do was check. Scotty really didn't give a shit if they ever scored. But here's the thing: They became something more than a checking line. They did score a little bit, and I think that came from them getting a little confidence from practicing every day against the best players in the world."

It all sounds perfectly reasonable, eh? But here's the thing: none of those four players remember any such a lecture from Bowman, either individually, in pairs or in a group of three or four. Ever. Bowman, too, says he cannot recall meeting with them and actually spelling it out like Devellano described. But each one of those Grind Line members quickly conceded that they understood, in no uncertain terms, what their coach expected of them. They knew their marching orders and they accepted them. And that is the beauty, the genius of Mr. William Scott Bowman.

As a coach, he was a man of few words—but all of them spoke volumes to his players.

"Did he ever sit us down? He never really had to," Draper said.

"As the Grind Line, we knew what we were supposed to do. Just like the Russian Five brought the finesse and the elite skill, our job was the exact opposite: Bring the pugilism, the physicality, the speed, the forecheck."

On their best nights, the Draper line could take away difficult matchups for Yzerman or Fedorov. They could skate with Joe Sakic and Peter Forsberg in Colorado, with Mike Modano and Joe Nieuwendyk in Dallas. And they could make life miserable for top-end defensemen like Chris Pronger and Al MacInnis in St. Louis.

"If we were able to do that," Draper said, "we knew it was a win for our team—and for our line."

And the Grind Line won more than its share of matchups, which is how they so quickly earned Bowman's confidence. Draper credits an uncommon bond with his linemates that they all seemed to recognize almost immediately. A single unified mission. One common goal.

"Three guys, one brain," is how Darren McCarty described it.

Chemistry, that ethereal trait that's nearly impossible to describe, yet athletes can feel—and smart coaches can recognize.

"It's amazing how some lines work and some don't," Draper said. "When the three of us started playing together, we immediately became best friends, not only on the ice but off the ice as well. We'd pull into wherever we'd go on the road, and we're all going to dinner—the three of us and whoever else. But always the three of us (and later four, when Kocur and McCarty became interchangeable on the right wing).

"Whether it was Joey or Mac on the right wing, we didn't miss a beat," Maltby said. "That system we played, with the left wing lock, we knew what the other guys were supposed to be doing, and it became easier to read plays."

"We just clicked," Draper added. "Then we kind of felt Scotty trusting us. That's something that, as an athlete, a hockey player, when you feel like the coach trusts you, all of a sudden you get to play with confidence."

That's not to say it was always just so. "Sure, we had our ups and down," Draper said. "We could get a little comfortable, but Scotty made sure that didn't last long."

And when the coach was angry at his team, the Grind Liners braced themselves. Bowman rarely singled out his top players for criticism in front of the group. But he had no problem calling out others.

"What's he going to do if things aren't going well?" Draper asked. "It was going to be attack mode at us, and we knew it. He knew he could make us uncomfortable, that we could handle it."

Taking one for the team. That was as much a part of the Grind Line's role as checking and killing penalties.

"For the most part, we knew we were a line that Scotty really trusted," Draper added.

———————————

Brendan Shanahan liked to talk about how enjoyable it was to sit on the bench and watch the Russian Five humiliate other teams with their uncanny puck-handling. Keep away. Always finding the open man because somehow, one of the five was always open. Pass after pass after tape-to-tape pass until, as Steve Yzerman describes it, someone eventually just passed it into an open net for a goal.

It looked like so much fun, Shanahan said, that Detroit's other lines started to embrace the same mentality: it's our puck, why let the other team have it? So began the era of puck-possession hockey in the copycat NHL. With a notable exception, it turns out.

"You know who was a huge fan of ours? Igor Larionov," Draper said. "That gave us so much confidence. In practice, he'd always

be telling us, 'Hold onto the puck. Try to make a play. Try to score.
. . You guys work so hard in the defensive zone. You get the puck
and get it to center ice. Why do you always get rid of it like that?'
And I'd say, 'Well, Igor, that's kind of our job. Get the puck from
the defensive zone to the offensive zone, so you guys can do your
thing. That's the object.'"

But there was that one time. . .

"Oh I remember one night, I came up over center ice and I was
kind of boxed out," Draper said. "I took a look, the team was on a
line change, so I circled back to the defense. We go D-to-D with the
puck, and we're good to go."

Doubtless the right play at the right moment. For the
wrong coach.

"I came back to the bench, and Scotty just lit into me," Draper
said, able at laugh now as he retells the story. "You don't regroup!
You don't play like the Russian Five! You get the puck and dump it
in, then get on the forecheck! Do you understand?'"

"I get it, Scotty. Loud and clear."

Hold on to the puck? Try to make a play? Not the Grind Line.

The power play is one of the most important weapons in every
team's arsenal. Gaining a manpower advantage and making the
best of it. It's crucial all the time, and critical in the playoffs, when
even-strength opportunities shrink. But practicing the power play
is one of the most difficult drills in the NHL because the man-ad-
vantage units are competing against their own team's penalty killers who, unlike opposing teams, know the precise strategy coaches
are trying to deploy.

In the late 1990s, which included those back-to-back Stanley
Cup seasons, Detroit had a devastating power play. With Hall of

Famers at nearly every position, how could they not? But practice? This was where Draper and Maltby had their most fun.

"Malts and I would look at one another, and we're like, 'We're going to piss these guys off today,'" Draper said. They'd be going against a line of perhaps Yzerman, Shanahan and Larionov, with Fedorov and Lidstrom on the points, and drive them all nuts. "Shutting those guys down, that was our win," Draper added. "And we knew Scotty loved it.

"Even in practice, we would block shots. We would hunt pucks. We would break something up. The whistle would go, and Malts and I would race down and score the shorty and just piss everybody off."

It has often been said that the Grind Liners became so much better because, as Devellano noted, they were practicing every day against some of the world's greatest players. Perhaps it's worth suggesting here that one of the reasons Detroit's power play units were so good in those days was because they were practicing against some of the best penalty killers in the world. Like iron knives sharpening one another.

So it was when the Red Wings practiced defensive coverage, which they did a lot under Bowman. "People probably underestimated how hard we worked in the defensive zone," Draper said. "Scotty didn't need to teach guys. They already elite hockey minds. So it ended up with some great battles."

For the Grind Line, the strategy didn't exactly involve rocket science. "It was protect the puck. Hold onto the puck. Make it harder for the other guys. That's where we started to gain the confidence. Man, you play five-on-five against the Russian Five down low, and you have the puck and you don't give it up to them, that's pretty good. Or you go one-on-one against Stevie, and you can hold onto the puck. . . It's those kinds of things in the late '90s and early 2000s that were huge growing moments—for all of us."

All that knife-sharpening would pay off at the most critical moments—almost as if Scotty Bowman had planned it that way. Less than six minutes into Game 1 of the Stanley Cup Final in Philadelphia, the Wings found themselves shorthanded when Tomas Sandstrom went off for high-sticking. Philadelphia coach Terry Murray, Bryan's younger brother, sent out his top power play unit, the Legion of Doom line with Rod Brind'Amour and Hall of Famer and ex-Wing Paul Coffey on the points.

"And then there's Malts and Drapes," Draper said, recalling the moment with perfect clarity. "We made a great play in the neutral zone, and we wound up having a two-on-none breakaway. I could have scored it, but I chipped it back to Malts for a one-timer, and he buried it for a 1-0 lead. All of a sudden, you could feel it. We could skate with this team."

Later, with just more than four minutes to play in the period, Joe Kocur intercepted an all-advised pass attempt by defenseman Janne Niinimaa and scored the prettiest goal of his career. He skated in alone from the blue line, deked the goaltender and nonchalantly roofed a backhander into the net.

"Looked like a fifty-goal man," Canadian TV broadcaster Bob Cole said.

"Looked like he was still playing in a beer league," Yzerman said.

"Looked like he learned a little something in that beer league," Holland said.

Regardless, the Wings took a rather comfortable 2-1 lead into the first intermission. The Grind Line had set the tone for the series. The Flyers were reeling, and the rout was on.

Battle Cry

As clearly as it happened yesterday, Kris Draper remembers when the Grind Line went from a cute, catchy nickname to-a rallying cry and ultimately an iconic identity. The Red Wings were in Phoenix, playing the Coyotes at the old America West Arena, the worst arena among NHL teams by a mile. The building was designed for NBA's Phoenix Suns long before the region entertained the thought of an NHL franchise.

The only good thing happening for the Wings that night was that more than half the crowd was wearing red and white and cheering wildly for the visiting team. (The Red Wings always travel well.) Otherwise—as sometimes happens to northern teams passing through the Sun Belt—not much else was going well. All that sunshine can have an adverse affect. Whatever the reason, the Wings were struggling. Except for the Grind Line.

"We had some shifts," Draper said. "We were playing against (Jeremy) Roenick, cycling the puck, hitting, and just kept coming at them. We felt good."

After one particularly good early shift, Draper made it known to anyone within earshot.

"I'll never forget that," Draper said. "We were on the bench and

I said something like, 'Boys, the Grind Line is going tonight!' And I said it kinda loud. I mean, come on. Who calls the Grind Line out in the third person like that, you know? We were sitting there waiting, and then we got the tap on our shoulder that we're going again."

And as they were jumping over the boards, changing on the fly, it came. That first battle cry. "We just yelled, 'Grind Line, go!' and we went out and did the same thing." Intense forechecking, cycling pucks, hitting anything that moved. It was contagious.

"Then everyone else ended up going, too, and we were able to go from not playing well to gathering some momentum, to getting a lot of momentum," Draper said. "What we were able to do was tread water until the big boys were kind of dragged into it. We lived for those moments."

And no one, aside from their coach, appreciated them more than big guns who were always under pressure to carry the offense.

"I can't speak for the Steves or Sergeis on our team," Maltby said, "but they were always expected to score—and it's really hard to score goals in the NHL. We knew Stevie was always going to be good. We knew our top guys would be good. But there are games when it's just not going to happen for them, whether they're snake-bitten, or the matchups are tough, or maybe it's back-to-back games and everyone's kind of lagging a little. I think we collectively felt as a line that if we could help change the momentum in a positive way for us, just go out physically, crash the net, maybe draw a penalty and get our power play out there. I mean, we could score some goals here or there, too, but there were a lot of other ways to help our team."

Whenever a team gets a goal from its bottom six forwards or the third defense pair, it can be an enormous lift, again especially for those who are always expected to score. "It allows them to just relax and go out and play their game," Maltby said, "not grip the stick a little harder, always thinking, 'We have to score!' Now they can just go out and just play their game. That's a big difference."

Perhaps no one bought into the Grind Line mystique more than the guy who built the unit. Scotty Bowman loved them, and they knew it.

"Scotty knew what we could do because of our mentality," Draper said. "There would be times when there might be twenty seconds left in a power play and we'd get the nod. And we're like, 'Oh boy, Scotty likes us tonight!'"

As the playoffs grew nearer, the Draper line's standing on the team seemed to grow exponentially. It wasn't uncommon for Bowman to announce his starting lineup quickly and characteristically gruffly: "Lidstrom, Murphy, Grind Line."

"We thrived off that," Draper said. "We were able to create that identity for ourselves, and Scotty let that identity grow."

Nevertheless, they were more than stunned—with just about everyone else—to get that call before Game 1 of the 1997 Stanley Cup Final in Philadelphia.

"Everyone was talking about Philadelphia's size and strength, and everyone was questioning us again," Draper said, acknowledging all the criticisms about being too small, too European, especially against a team lead by Eric Lindros and his mammoth line. "Everybody is talking and writing about how it's going to be Yzerman vs. Lindros, with (Vladimir) Konstantinov and (Slava) Fetisov on defense. The media had it all lined up."

And all so very wrong.

"Starting lineup," Bowman said after the pregame warm-up, "Nick, Murph, Grind Line."

"Typical Scotty," Draper said. "Everyone expects that I'm going this way, so I'm doing this instead. Obviously, he wanted Swede and Murphy for puck possession, to get the puck out of our zone

144/ *The Grind Line*

quickly. And he wanted us to use our speed and go against Lindros, LeClair and Renberg."

Bowman's starting announcement came at the last minute, just as the players were lining up to take the ice. No time to think about it. "Thank goodness," Draper said.

According to tradition, the starting goaltender, Mike Vernon, led the team out onto the ice, and the five starting skaters filed out last. While all the other players headed to the Detroit bench, the starters skated to the blue line to await the National Anthem. Still some time for some personal contemplation.

"The starting lineup. Man, this is something," Draper thought. "Of all the options Scotty had and. . . It all comes back to the trust he had in us. It was something that we never, ever took for granted."

As they got ready for the opening face-off, Draper gripping his stick at center ice, McCarty adjusting his elbow pads, and Maltby already jockeying for position on the circle, the Grind Line didn't say a word. But Draper's eyes spoke volumes to his mates: "Boys, I need to win this draw, we've got to get in on the puck, on the fore-check, just establish what we do and frustrate Eric right away. That's the mindset we had to have. It's what Scotty had."

And it's what the Grind Line delivered. Draper won the face off and the Wings were off and running.

"We throw the puck in and, boom! Maltby hits somebody," said Brendan Shanahan, who was watching from the bench. "The puck goes D-to-D and then, boom! McCarty hits somebody. . . In the first minute and a half, we were quicker, heavier, meaner and hit harder."

Truth be told, the Flyers didn't seem to know what hit them. They played as though they were dazed and confused—especially after Grind Liners Maltby and Kocur gave Detroit a 2-1 well before the first period ended. And suddenly—it didn't take long—all those who predicted a rather smooth Stanley Cup ride for the big, bad Flyers began to wonder: hmmm, what's happening here?

When the Grind Line came back to the bench after that first shift, Bowman leaned over, put his hand on Draper's shoulder, and said, "When Lindros gets up, you guys be ready to go."

Oh, they were ready.

Grind Line, go!

The rest is history.

An Opposing Point of View

Mike Modano had a love-hate relationship with his hometown team. He got steady diet of the Grind Line and he hated every minute of it. But he loved playing against the Red Wings for the pure joy of the competition.

The Westland, Michigan native and first overall pick in the 1988 NHL Entry Draft, Modano played a central role in one of the most contentious eras in the history of the league. From the mid-1990s to the early 2000s, The Detroit-Colorado rivalry transcended all National Hockey League storylines. But frankly, Modano's Dallas Stars were every bit the equal to both those Western Conference powers, and the only team in the East that could match those three with any consistency was New Jersey. For nine straight seasons, the Stanley Cup would go to one of those four teams, and for the first eight of those seasons, either Detroit (four times), Colorado or Dallas (twice each) were in the Cup Final:

> 1995 – New Jersey over Detroit
> 1996 – Colorado over Florida
> 1997 – Detroit over Philadelphia
> 1998 – Detroit over Washington

1999 – Dallas over Buffalo
2000 – New Jersey over Dallas
2001 – Colorado over New Jersey
2002 – Detroit over Carolina
2003 – New Jersey Anaheim

The Dallas-Colorado rivalry was every ounce as competitive as Detroit-Colorado, though not nearly as hateful and vicious. And the Detroit-Dallas rivalry was equally worth the price of admission in those years. The 1998 Western Conference Final between Detroit and Modano's Stars was by far the most competitive and entertaining series of the entire playoffs. And nasty, too. Who can forget Dallas goaltender Eddie Belfour bringing his stick up hard—like he was trying to set the hook on shark—between Martin Lapointe's legs?

Detroit won the series in six games, prevailing on the strength of Mike Vernon's goaltending (two shutouts) and the checking acumen of the Grind Line, which limited Modano to just one goal among four points in the six games. In Modano's defense, the reason he couldn't escape the Grind Line's blanket coverage was because the Stars' other Hall of Fame center, Joe Nieuwendyk, missed the series because of a knee injury he suffered in the opening five minutes of the playoffs that spring.

Modano, Wings fans may recall, ended his career as a Red Wing, signing with the club for the 2010-11 season. A severe skate cut to his wrist limited him to just forty games. And, in a disgustingly cruel move by coach Mike Babcock, Modano was a healthy scratch for the final game of the season—preventing him from playing in his 1,500th career game before his planned retirement. But Modano remains beloved in Dallas, where the Stars not only recognized his Hall of Fame career by retiring his No. 9, but also resurrected a statue in his honor outside their American Airlines Arena.

Like Steve Yzerman, Modano confesses to having the most difficulty with opponents who could skate with him. And there weren't many. Modano was one of the smoothest, fastest skaters in the world in his era, but he could never seem to shed Draper. "Kris was such a good skater, he could defend well, and he was really good in the face-off circle—and all those guys on that line were really smart."

The Grind Line was different than most checking lines of that generation, which typically featured size, toughness and brute force.

"Those were actually guys who could really play and contribute and be a big factor in games," Modano said in an August interview from his home in Minnesota, where he is executive adviser to Wild GM Bill Guerin. "They could score, check, win big draws, defend and close games out. A couple of them were penalty killers. The combination, they just really checked all the boxes."

Included in their game, Modano and other opponents pointed out, was a healthy dose of chirping and the more than occasional cheap shot—because with Joe Kocur or Darren McCarty on the other wing, they knew they could get away with it.

"Oh yeah, those guys weren't dumb, that's for sure,' Modano said. "They knew they had some good backup looking over their shoulder, knowing they could push the envelope a little bit, try to get guys off their game in different ways. They always had the muscle behind them if things did get sideways."

After Detroit won back-to-back titles in 1997-98, Dallas advanced to the Cup Final the following two years, each time defeating Colorado in the Western Conference Final. Each time, the Avs advanced by ending Detroit's season, then they took the Stars to the limit both years.

"To this day, those two seven-game series with Colorado was some of the best hockey I ever experienced," Modano said. "Still, it would have been fun to cross paths with Detroit in '99 and 2000.

Those series were amazing. Prison rules. Hitting, slashing, hacking. My God, some of the stuff was just vicious."

Today's NHL game, while entertaining to watch, Modano said, pales in comparison to the intensity of competition in his era. "You can't resurrect what we went through in those late '80s and '90s series," he said. "Now it's all skill and high-octane up and down the ice. Guys come through the neutral zone at a hundred miles an hour and don't get touched. When we tried that we'd be dragging five guys with us."

And while today's NHL might be enjoyable to some, Modano misses a time when the game featured some real characters, guys like Brett Hull and Darren McCarty. "The players are so robotic now. You just don't have the personalities as some guys back then. No one seems to have a good time anymore. No one laughs or has fun. It's so money-driven now."

A couple of Grind Liners might well agree with that assessment. McCarty was sitting up in the press box with Draper during the 2023-24 season, watching as the Red Wings blew a huge lead and lost a game in overtime to the dreadful San Jose Sharks. Yeah, it was maddening for them to watch, too. Cost them a chance to make the playoffs.

"How the fuck do you blow a four-goal lead?" McCarty asked.

"Dude, you watch the games," Draper responded. "Does anybody hit anybody anymore?"

They sure did when the Grind Line was trying to corral Mike Modano in some of the best of times in Hockeytown.

A Wrong Number?

Assistant coach Barry Smith learned the hard way about the perils labeling players, however innocent his intentions. He and fellow assistant Dave Lewis were discussing their team with coach Scotty Bowman when Smith casually mentioned the team's fourth line.

He hadn't yet completed his sentence when Bowman curtly interrupted him. "Scotty jumped down his throat," is how Lewis remembered it.

"What the hell are you talking about Barry? Fourth line? What's that?" Bowman barked. "You mean the Draper line? Is that what you mean? Then say it!"

Bowman was on to something. Then again, Scotty Bowman is always on to something. This time, his message was loud and clear. To refer to the Draper line—the Grind Line as it had come to be known around the NHL—as the fourth line was a disservice to the players on that forward unit, bordering on being disrespectful.

"They were not a fourth line," Doug MacLean said adamantly. The former Wings assistant coach and general manager, who later coached against Detroit and the Grind Line when he was with the Florida Panthers, knew what the rest of the NHL would soon figure out. "That was a good second line on most teams, at worst a second-and-a-half line. They became as important as any line in the league."

At the same time, it's impossible to ignore the hierarchy of Detroit's star-studded lineup. Draper had three Hall of Famers ahead of him at center. To start numbering them risks having to label captain Steve Yzerman as a third-liner. Or Igor Larionov. Sergei Fedorov was the best hockey player in the world in those back-to-back Stanley Cup seasons in the late 1990s—Detroit's top center and, arguably, its second-best defenseman.

"You didn't just coach players on that team, you coached egos," Lewis said. "That was something Scotty managed really well. Whether he managed or just didn't care, it's what he did, and they accepted it."

Oh, Bowman cared. That's why he was careful about labels.

"No numbers on the lines. That was a key," Lewis said. "If we needed a goal, he knew who to put on the ice. If you want to maintain, that's the Grind Line. Whatever the situation was, he knew who to play. And the players? They not only accepted their roles but they took pride in what they did."

Pull Yzerman off the ice and insert Draper because the Wings needed a left-handed face-off specialist? Bowman did it often. Pull Joe Kocur or Darren McCarty off the ice and replace them with Yzerman on the Grind Line? Bowman did that often, too, putting Detroit's two best face-off men on the ice at the same time—in case one of them got thrown out of the circle by the official.

"Whatever Scotty did, it was accepted by everybody," Lewis said. "You didn't have to have a private meeting with one or two of them to explain why we did this or that. Everybody just knew."

They also knew that Bowman, except in rare circumstances, matched opponents' top lines with his top defense pairing, which in those days was Nick Lidstrom and Larry Murphy. Bowman also didn't get too attached to his forward lines. Rather, he liked to find a center and a winger who could play well and responsibly together and he would often change out the second winger for whatever might be needed at the time.

Draper and Kirk Maltby were attached at the hip, of course. So were Larionov and Brendan Shanahan. Fedorov, when he wasn't on Larionov's wing with the Russian Five, would center a line with Doug Brown. And Yzerman?

"It didn't matter," Lewis said, acknowledging that the captain often paired with veteran Tomas Sandstrom. "Whoever played with Stevie, he made them better."

But the Grind Line, with either Kocur or McCarty on Draper's right wing, reached a special level of recognition and trust from their coach. For good reason.

"This was a line that contributed to Stanley Cups. That's what they did. They were that important," MacLean said. "It was a special line. They had speed. They had hockey sense. They had toughness. And when you have those elements, especially with that speed. . . They shut down the other teams' best players. Not only that, they made big plays, scored important goals.

"The Grind Line has as good a reputation, in my opinion, as Philadelphia's Legion of Doom line because they were winners. They. Were. Winners."

———◆———

Gordie Howe, always careful to give credit where it's due, was fond of saying the Red Wings never would have won those four Stanley Cups in the 1950s without Marty Pavelich the speedy, diminutive checking center. (Think Kris Draper 1.0). Yzerman says the same thing about the importance of the Grind Line to the teams he captained.

"For sure," Yzerman acknowledged in an interview during training camp in Traverse City, moments after locking up defenseman Mo Seider on a seven-year contract. "The Grind Line was good. They were a pain in the ass to play against. They were on you, on you, on you, and they would score some goals against you.

"You look back at those playoff runs, that line, at some point in an important game in each series, scored a big goal. And they came up big in the Finals against the Flyers, especially in that Game 1. They just balanced our team better. Good penalty killers. Good checkers. And a lot of speed. That line was integral to our team."

And speaking as a general manager, Yzerman offered another perspective: "In today's NHL, they would be an elite third line."

Interestingly, in either iteration—either Kocur or McCarty on the right wing—the players were at their best as a unit.

"When you separated them, they weren't as effective," said Lewis, who succeeded Bowman as coach in 2002 and still owns the best win percentage (.672) of anyone who has coached more than 100 Wings games. "It had to do with confidence maybe, their comfort level in their own skin on that line. Really, it was the difference between all-star caliber and just a regular fourth-line player, and that helped their careers, too. When you see success like that, the chemistry and pride that those guys had to deliver, it was so good. It was fun coaching a line like that."

To be sure, there have been similarly successful units through the NHL's recent history. New Jersey's Crash Line helped to sweep Detroit in the 1995 Final, though it falls far short of the Grind Line in speed and overall skill. Edmonton's Kid Line in 1990, with former Red Wings Adam Graves and Joe Murphy, with Martin Gelinas, added a certain energetic dimension, young, fast and skilled. Though they hardly could be considered a true checking line. And both those were rather short-lived combinations.

In the foreword to this book, Bowman noted perhaps the first true elite checking line that made so much difference to the dynasty the Montreal Canadians built in the late 1970s, with Doug Risebrough centering Mario Tromblay and Yvon Lambert. But they didn't match the longevity of the Grind Line, featured in Bowman's lineup for five seasons, followed by two more years with Lewis behind the bench. The line was reunited for parts of two seasons after McCarty's comeback, including the 2008 Cup run under Mike Babcock.

Barry Smith wasn't wrong in referring to the Draper line as the team's fourth line in those days. Of course it was, given the talent on those teams. But given all that it accomplished over more than a decade in which the Detroit Red Wings were the best team in the league, would it be wrong to suggest that the Grind Line represents the greatest fourth line in National Hockey League history? Let the debate begin, though you'll get no argument from Kris Draper.

"I would gladly take that," he said. "I'll take that all day long."

'No wonder we couldn't ever score
against the Grind Line.
There were four of you assholes!'

~ Kelly Chase
former St. Louis Blues enforcer,
to his boyhood friend, Joe Kocur

Grindstones

In the earliest days of the Grind Line, after all his years of service, Joe Kocur had finally found a home on a unit his coach seemed to like. Darren McCarty, meantime, was living the good life on Steve Yzerman's right wing, even getting power play time.

Depending on the situation, coach Scotty Bowman would occasionally give McCarty a shift on the Grind Line—which he enjoyed, especially when the line started to gain some notoriety with its fancy new nickname and the cool T-shirts that fans were buying as fast as the team could produce them.

"Oh, Mac loved playing with Yzerman. Of course he did," Kris Draper said, "but he really wanted to be on that T-shirt, too. We always kid him about that."

Can you blame him?

"When you mention the Grind Line, everybody in the NHL knows who that is," McCarty said. "It's like the Production Line. We don't need the Hall of Fame. Everybody knows the Russian Five, the Production Line and the Grind Line. The ones who matter, they all know. And we all knew that everyone in that (dressing) room, that entire organization, they appreciated us."

And they had the T-shirts to prove it.

The ninth hole on The Links course at the Bay Harbor Golf Club
in Petoskey is a picturesque 490-yard par 5 with Joe Kocur's name
on it. Seriously, there is a plaque near the tee box proclaiming: "Joe
Kocur, #26, holed a 6-iron from this location on September 8, 1999,
to record the first double eagle at Bay Harbor Golf Club."

Photo courtesy of Bay Harbor Golf Club

The plaque commemorating Joe Kocur's historic albatross at one of
northern Michigan's iconic golf clubs.

Kocur used a 3-wood off the tee for a drive that hugged the
hazard to the right and made for a far easier approach to a wonder-
fully contoured green. "Then I knocked a 6-iron in for a double
eagle," he said, rather nonchalantly considering a double-eagle—
also known as an albatross—is one of the rarest events in golf. Odds
makers put it at something like six million to one. For perhaps a
better understanding, consider that in his professional career Tiger

Woods has had 20 aces, holes in one, but he has never recorded a double-eagle.

For the record, there has been just one albatross recorded at Bay Harbor since Kocur's, according to Ken Griffin, Bay Harbor's director of golf sales and marketing. It was accomplished on the same ninth hole by a club member, Griffin said.

―――――――――――

Draper admits to playing most of his career with a big chip on his shoulder. Most of his life, in fact.

In a story he penned for *The Players' Tribune*, Draper took readers all the way back to Career Day in Grade Six in West Hill, Ontario. He recalled how the teacher went around the room asking all the students what they wanted to be when they grew up. And there were would-be doctors, lawyers, teachers, firefighters, veterinarians, etc. Then the teacher pointed to Draper.

"I'm going to play in the NHL," he said, and that's when it started.

"I was a small kid, so there was some laughter in the room," Draper wrote. "After school was over, I was sitting outside on the portable step, and I'll never forget this as long as I live: this kid (who shall remain nameless), came up to me and said, 'Ha! You'll never play in the NHL.'

"Just the way he said it, with such certainty, always stuck with me. I used it as motivation. I'd picture his face, and just the way he said it, and I'd think, Oh yean? I'll show you."

And he did. He showed all of us, eh?

―――――――――――

Two days away from his sixth birthday, Griffin McCarty is playing mini-sticks with his old man, when there's a pause in the action, enough time to ask a quick question.

"Dude, it's your big on Monday. What do you want for your birthday?"

It was an innocent and important question. But it wasn't like Darren McCarty had a lot of time for shopping just then. He and his teammates were about to face the Colorado Avalanche in the 2002 Western Conference Finals. It didn't matter that half the Detroit roster would wind up in the Hockey Hall of Fame one day; it would be a monumental challenge to beat the embittered archrivals and advance to the Stanley Cup Final for the third time in six seasons.

"Score a goal for me, Dad."

Now McCarty is taken aback, not quite sure how to respond. He wasn't paid to score goals. He had just five in 62 games all season. I'm on the Grind Line. Our job is to keep the puck out of our net.

"Whoa, whoa, whoa, Son. I don't want to disappoint you, but I'm not sure I should promise you that. It's not the name on the back, it's the crest on the front, remember?

The boy looked at his father with his worshipful eyes and quietly said, "Stevie would have said yes."

Those words crushed the man Griffin McCarty most admired. Fast forward two days. The Red Wings are down, 3-2, going into the third period. McCarty takes a pass from defenseman Chris Chelios and rifles it over Patrick Roy's shoulder to tie it up. Then he scored again on an assist from Kirk Maltby, a goal McCarty describes as his second favorite ever behind the Stanley Cup-winning goal against Philadelphia in 1997.

"I'm with Kirk, who by the way is the greatest decoy ever, which he knows. I'm the shooter, right? Just don't give me the puck until I can shoot it. So I'm going down the wing–that was my routine after every practice, hit that shot. This one I couldn't have hit any better. Slapper. Short side. Bar down. It was a surreal moment."

But he wasn't done yet. He scored one more time, completing the natural hat trick, three consecutive goals, the only one in his NHL career, on a rebound of a Maltby shot.

Wings win. Grind Line again sets the tone for another all-important series. But the best part about that day, McCarty recalls, is coming off the ice. The first person he sees is Griffin, and he gave his son a bear hug.

"Hey Bud, I didn't get you one. I got you three. Hope you're not mad."

"Dad, that was the best birthday present ever!"

And Darren McCarty gave his son the same look Griffin gave his dad a few days before and said, "Stevie would have only got you one.

"Now please, don't ever ask me to do that again."

Joe Kocur will be forever grateful to Scotty Bowman for giving him a kind of home on a line that made him feel, for the first time ever, like an actual NHL regular, and not just a role player whose main gig was to beat guys up. But he knows the score.

"I got into the league for a reason, and I'll be honest with you, I stayed in the league for a reason," he said. "I wasn't staying around for any other skill. I'm known for that, and I should be known for that, so I'm not disappointed."

That said, he wouldn't mind a little respect in describing his role.

"I'm sure if you asked Probie, if he were still alive, or Dave Semenko or anybody like that, do we like the word 'enforcer?' A hundred percent," he said. "But I don't care for some of the other words."

He loathes terms like goon, thug, cement head, or any other pejorative labels often used for those one-dimensional physical players. But enforcer? He's good with that. Mr. Kocur also works. That's how a lot of people around the NHL were referring to him after a notable fight with Winnipeg's Jim Kyte, one of the toughest players in the league in his time. "Not to say I was any tougher, but I was lucky enough to get in that one good shot," Kocur recalled. And what a shot.

Kyte crumpled to the ice, and he was out cold. Contrary to most scenes like that at The Joe, you could suddenly hear a pin drop. Former Wings trainer Jim Pengelly was the first one on the ice to get to Kyte. After one of the more memorable fights of 219 over his fifteen-year-career, Kocur skated away in eerie silence.

"Usually when you win a fight like that, your teammates are all high-fiving you," Kocur said. "When I skated off, nobody even looked at me. They were all looking at him laying there on the ice, not moving, almost like they were in shock."

Five for fighting. . . Mr. Kocur. Kyte recovered, was helped off the ice and didn't return.

As we were discussing how much the game has changed from those years to now, how very different it is from a law and order perspective, Kocur recalled a time when Rick Tocchet, the renowned power forward and tough guy then playing for Washington, was sent to the penalty box for a cheap shot on Steve Yzerman's knees.

"One of the few times I was ever out on a penalty kill," Kocur said. "Scotty sent me out to kill the last 20 seconds, and when it ended I was basically standing at the penalty box. Tocchet came out of the box, dropped his gloves and we had a go.

"He looked at me like, 'I know why you're here. I know what I did, and I know the punishment. Let's get it over with. And we did."

Code.

All but gone in today's game.

One of the many life lessons Darren McCarty learned in the years that he played for Scotty Bowman was this: "In this lifetime, you will be somebody's bitch. That's a fact."

McCarty and his teammates saw that in action on an everyday basis in the way Bowman treated his associate coach, Barry Smith. A universally and highly respected coach throughout hockey, and the author of Detroit's famed left-wing lock defensive scheme, Smith was also Bowman's favorite whipping boy. But the kind and easygoing Smith had an enormous capacity to just roll with it. He had been at Bowman's side long before the two arrived in Detroit. He knew his role as a bit of a lightning rod when Bowman's mood needed one.

"Barry was Scotty's bitch," McCarty said. "If Scotty wanted to yell at you on the bench, he'd stand behind you, with Barry to his right, and yell, 'Barry, you tell McCarty that if he ever does that again, he'll never play another fucking shift for me!' Then he'd walk away and Barry would lean over and say, 'Did you catch that?' And I'd go, 'Oh yeah. You think I can't fucking hear?' Barry knew his role."

Now the natural extension of this lesson, McCarty said, is that we all have to ask ourselves: Whose bitch am I? He eventually figured that out, too.

"It took me three years of sucking my thumb in the corner for me to figure it out, but Steve Yzerman fucking owns me," McCarty said. "To this day, I mean I ran into him at a game the other night, and it all came back to me. It was all there again."

More than likely, that feeling stems from the overwhelming need to please his captain or at the very least not to disappoint him either on or off the ice.

"To his credit, I know he always wanted the best for me," McCarty said. "But what he's seen from guys like Probie. . . and me.

That's when it hits you: How lucky am I. Fifteen years later, to have Steve Yzerman and all these guys who know me to the core—him, Drapes, Joey – and they just want me to be happy. But still to this day, that feeling never changes."

Every now and then, a major individual trophy can feel a tiny bit like a team award. At least that's how Maltby felt when the guy attached to his right hip throughout his career in Detroit won the Selke Trophy as the NHL's best defensive forward.

Kris Draper established career highs with twenty-four goals among forty points in sixty-seven games in 2003-04, the fourth time in an eleven-year span that a Detroit player had won the award. (Sergei Fedorov won in 1994 and 1996 and Steve Yzerman won in 2000.) Which speaks volumes for the style of play that helped Detroit win three Stanley Cup titles in that span.

"One of the things I'm proudest of, without sounding like a dad or anything, was Drapes winning that Selke Trophy," Maltby said. "Drapes and I stuck up for each other. We helped each other. Full marks for him not just for career highs scoring goals and so on, but again, it all goes back to being responsible defensively, playing the right way.

"In that regard, I was over the moon happy for him."

Kris Draper didn't make the NHL roster in his first training camp with the Red Wings, which ticks him off to this day, but he certainly succeeded in making a good impression.

Not only did he win the Iron Man Award as the best-conditioned player who reported to camp, but on the ice he made a good first impression as well.

"You start to watch him, and you can't help but see he's a really good skater, and he has a pretty good shot," said Lewis. "Maybe not a great stickhandler, but he had no problem with the puck. Honestly, we couldn't understand what the faults to his game were. To this day, I can't understand what happened in Winnipeg."

The one obvious blemish to his game, and this might be a stretch, was skating in alone on the goaltender. "Seemed like he got a breakaway a game," Lewis said. "And when he did, Scotty would always lean over and say, 'He's not scoring.' Sure enough, he wouldn't score. But that wasn't his role on that team."

Kelvington, Saskatchewan, Joe Kocur's hometown, was named for Lord William Thomson Kelvin, a Scottish-Irish physicist and one of the most eminent scientists of the 19th century. He is best known for inventing the international system of absolute temperature that bears his name, the Kelvin Scale.

The Kelvinator Company, which produces refrigerators, was founded in Detroit in 1914. The irony is not lost on the kid from Kelvington.

"How curious," Kocur said in his book, "that a young lad from the town named after Kelvin would also make a name for himself in the Motor City by knocking people out cold?"

Spend as much time on the road as the Red Wings did in those days when they were the only Eastern-time-zone club in the NHL's Western Conference, and it's little wonder that some of their favorite memories have little to do with hockey.

"We really did have a lot of long road trips, and when you spend that much time together, it really does tend to turn back the clock on you," said Kirk Maltby. "You become that little minor hockey kid when you and your buddies are sleeping over at a tournament and you're playing mini-sticks."

Malty recalled a time when they were in a hotel and there was some pranking going on. As he was prone to do, Chris Osgood was in the middle of it all—him and his roommate Draper.

In response, Maltby said, he and Kocur "moved one of those pop (vending) machines and put it in front of their door. They could open their door because it opened into the room, but they couldn't get out.

"You have no idea how heavy those machines are. It definitely helped having Joey around. He was most of the muscle behind moving that thing."

There's more. So much more. That's the really good stuff, Maltby said.

"Just stupid things like that, when you turn into little kids again. You're kind of giddy, just loving each other. Like family."

One of the biggest challenges Scotty Bowman faced as a coach in halcyon Stanley Cup years in Detroit was keeping his four elite center-ice men, Hall of Famers Steve Yzerman, Sergei Fedorov, Igor Larionov—and Kris Draper—happy with the amount of ice time they were getting.

"I was there when they started putting ice time on the score sheets," Bowman said. "And the minute those things came out, Victor (Fedorov) would get one. He had it in his mind that if Sergei didn't reach twenty minutes, then he was pissed off. The dad, he kind of wound Sergei up a bit.

"I sat him down and said, 'Sergei, this is what I can do.' That's why we moved him to defense. We had a couple of guys hurt, and I convinced him that he was going to get a lot of minutes."

Fedorov indeed racked up the minutes, and he played brilliantly on the blue line—hating every minute of it, while highlighting the skills that put him above some of the greatest players who ever played the game.

"I remember talking to Wayne Gretzky, much later on," Bowman said. "We were talking about Fedorov, and Wayne said, 'I could never have played defense. Mario (Lemieux) couldn't have. (Jaromir) Jagr couldn't have. You know, there aren't many guys who could skate backward like that.'"

A golden memory: In the past 35 years or so, I've had a string of eight golden retrievers. I fell in love with the breed back when I was covering the Red Wings for the *Free Press*. On the occasional weekend morning, coach Jacques Demers allowed his players to bring their dogs to the rink for a light practice. (He had no idea that some of them were letting their dogs pee in his office.)

Kocur brought his golden. Molson, of course. It was as close to love at first sight as I'd ever experienced.

"Were you at the rink when he jumped over the board onto the ice?" Kocur asked, laughing as he retold the story. That wasn't one of those casual Saturday workouts at the Joe. The Wings were at one of the suburban rinks they would sometimes use, likely in Oak Park. For reasons he can't remember, Kocur was forced to bring Molson with him to practice. Before the players went onto the ice, Kocur brought his dog into the dressing room, closed the door with strict instructions to the trainers: "Keep him in the goddamned locker room.

"Sure enough, somebody opened the door, and pretty soon Molson is on the ice in the middle of a drill."

Fast forward several years, to 2001, when Kocur was the video coach. He was preparing for a crucial game with Colorado when he got a phone call. Bowman could tell something was wrong.

"What's going on?" the coach asked.

"Molson died," Kocur said. "That was my wife. He's laying on the floor in my office."

"Get your ass home!"

"Scotty, I can't. We're playing Colorado. I'll take care of it later."

"Oh no. You've got to get home right now. Get moving!"

And with that, the coach pushed Kocur toward the door. Some things are more important than hockey, even for Scotty Bowman

———————————————

Speaking of big hearts, Kocur was in the process of buying a house, and he was depending on a sizable bonus he was owed to help cover the down payment. He had recently been traded by Detroit to the New York Rangers, but it was the Wings who owed him the bonus, and they kept putting him off. Finally, the bean counters told him he'd have to wait another month for the payment because they had too many other bonuses they had to pay out to the players on Detroit's roster.

Desperate, Kocur went to the top of the organization.

"Somehow, I got Mr. Ilitch's phone number, I don't even remember how, and I called him."

"Come see me tomorrow, and I'll write you a personal check," Ilitch told him. And the next day, after a brief, congenial visit, Kocur left Mike Ilitch with a check for $100,000 so he could close on his house.

"That's the type of guy he was," Kocur said. And the telling of that story triggered another one.

"We were in Los Angeles and had a great comeback in a game to win in overtime," Kocur said. "Mr. Ilitch came into the room afterward, and he was really fired up. 'That was the most fun I've had in a long time,' he said. 'Everybody in this room gets a $5,000 bonus. And Stevie, because you got the game winner, you get $10,000.'"

The captain used his extra 5K to buy a whole new stereo system for the Wings locker room, Kocur said.

One of the hardest things about winning is how abrupt it can all end. One minute you're raising hell with your best pals and quenching your thirst out of the Stanley Cup, and the next minute. . .

"The sad thing is what happens after the parades and all the other festivities," Maltby said. "Everyone just kind of goes their separate ways. We don't spend a lot of down time with each other during the offseason."

Golfing helps, especially on those rare occasions when a foursome includes the four guys on the Grind Line.

"We all love golf," Maltby said. "Mac was a good golfer, and of course when the newest, greatest thing that came out, whether it was a club or whatever, he would have to have it. And he always got it. But it didn't necessarily help his game."

Dave Lewis recalled the time McCarty showed up for a charity outing in a foursome that also included Craig Wolanin, the defenseman from Grosse Pointe who won a Stanley Cup with Colorado in 1996. This was well after all three had retired from the game. McCarty, his hair braided in red corn-rolls, greeted his group with an apology.

"I don't know how much I can help you guys today," he said.

"Why, what's the matter," Lewis responded.

"Well, I broke some ribs, three or four of 'em."

Turns out that a few days earlier, on a Saturday night, McCarty was wrestling in a show at the Fowlerville Fair. "Somebody threw me on a table, and the table didn't break properly," he said.

"Gees, Darren, you know you're not 25 anymore," Lewis told him. "But that's him. It's his DNA. He gutted out two rounds that day. With broken ribs."

The one beautiful thing about retiring and going into scouting with the club, Maltby said, has been access to information that heretofore had been relegated to the rumor mill or otherwise unsubstantiated media reports.

"I'd heard all the stories of when Scotty came in, the rumors that Stevie was getting traded to Ottawa," he said, adding that he had accepted most of that as just so much rumor and innuendo, since no one in the know around the league would dare to confirm that the talk was actually serious. "Then I sat in a lot of meetings, which would go on for hours on end, with Ken Holland and Jimmy Devellano. Those meetings probably lasted a day too long because of all the stories they had to tell."

And the one certainty Maltby came away with from those meetings and stories: "All that stuff about trading Stevie? Oh yeah. It almost happened."

Scotty Bowman didn't spend a whole lot of time meeting one on one with his players, but when he did he had an uncanny ability to get them to understand his point of view. And sometimes he could be unsettling.

"I can laugh at it now, but there was one time when we had this pretty intense meeting," Draper said. "All of a sudden, Scotty pauses and looks up at the ceiling, not saying anything."

Draper sat there, wondering if somehow the meeting was over and what he should say or do next, when the coach finally spoke.

"You know what?" Bowman said softly, almost as though he were speaking to himself. "The only thing that's permanent in this entire room is that light fixture up there."

To Draper, it felt like a dagger. "I was kind of like, 'OK Scotty. I get it. I understand."

Then the meeting was over.

When Joe Kocur returned to the Wings for his encore performance after spending some time in a local rec league, he was greeted warmly by his new Wings teammates. Except for that one time. . .

"Probably the second practice after I was back and we're doing a drill," Kocur recalled. "I'm going into the corner for the puck, and all of a sudden somebody fucking slams me from behind, and I go head first into the boards. I get up and took a look. 'Who's that?' It was (Tomas) Holmstrom. Now I'm not going to do anything to him. I didn't even know him. But I always wondered.

"I don't know how much later it was—it might even have been when I was a coach. Maybe we were at a bar. I can't remember for shit. But I finally asked him, 'Homer, why did you run me in that practice like you did right after I got back?' And he goes, 'You were taking my spot!' Just a matter of fact like that. And I said, 'You know what? I get it. I really respect that.'"

End of conversation. Such is life in the National Hockey League.

Not only were the Grind Line mates a coach's dream to work with, but they were some of the lowest-maintenance players in the Detroit locker room in those days. Sure, physical therapist saw a lot of

Draper, Maltby, Kocur and McCarty, but that's because the train-er's room was a favorite hangout for them. A place to have a cup of coffee, shoot the breeze and take a break from weight room.

"All four of those guys, as people and as hockey people, were just a joy to be around," Wharton said. "Some guys could get a bit curmudgeonly, almost like bipolar sometimes. But those guys never got too high. Never got too low. They were always just pleasant to be around. We'd be down, 3-2, they were always positive. They were like, 'there's no way we can lose this.' And their mentality was contagious in that room."

Of the four, Wharton figures he was closest to Draper. "And that's only because I spent time with him nearly every day after his jaw was wired shut because of that hit in Colorado. I wanted to make sure he was getting all the nourishment he needed—through a straw.

"All of them, really, just went about their business. Seriously, I hardly ever saw them except when they came in (to the trainer's room) to shoot the crap. But from a medical standpoint, all four of them? Very low maintenance."

One of Wharton's proudest memories from that 1997 Stanley Cup run: "I lost one man game due to injury. Joey had back spasms in Game Four in Anaheim, and he couldn't go. That's the only man game we lost."

———

Since two of the four Grind Liners were distinguished brawlers, and one of their celebrated teammates suffered a severe brain injury, it would be remiss not to at least raise the subject of CTE considering all those blows to the head.

After Bob Probert died at age forty-five of heart failure, Boston University researchers determined that he had the degenerative brain disease Chronic Traumatic Encephalopathy. The disease has also been found in the brains of other noted NHL enforcers—and athletes in other contact sports–after their deaths.

"We are only beginning to appreciate the consequences of brain trauma in sports," Chris Nowinski, the Sports Legacy Institute's co-founder and chief executive officer, told *The Associated Press.* "Early evidence indicates that the historical decision not to discourage contact to the head was an enormous mistake, and we hope aggressive changes continue to be made to protect athletes, especially at the youth level."

CTE, originally referred to as dementia pugilistica because it was thought to only affect boxers, is a progressive brain disease believed to be caused by repetitive trauma to the brain, including concussions or sub-concussive blows.

Head injuries have altered the careers of some of the game's biggest stars. Philadelphia Hall of Famer Eric Lindros left the game far earlier than he'd planned after a series of concussions. Keith Primeau, one of Probert's teammates in Detroit, was forced into early retirement in 2006 because of several concussions he sustained during his fifteen NHL seasons. Primeau has committed to donating his brain on his death.

Meantime, the subject of CTE is taboo for Tie Domi, who actually fought more than Probert in the same era. Domi is just fine not knowing, content to whistle past the graveyard, thank you very much. He doesn't need a doctor telling him what he doesn't want to know. And who can blame him?

"If I get checked out, then what?" asked Domi, in a story reported by the *Toronto Sun.* "What's that going to do for me?"Listen, I've got three kids that I live every day for. I can't be thinking about this. I don't want anybody worrying for me."

In Detroit, the CTE issue rarely surfaced during his time with the Wings, Wharton said, primarily because the science hadn't caught up with the sport.

"Obviously, it's talked about more now, as it should be, because we know so much more now than we did then," Wharton said. "Hindsight being 20-20, knowing what we do know, there are a lot of things we would have done differently."

Wharton recalled the collision involving Shawn Burr and Sergei Fedorov that kept Fedorov sideline several days and probably cost him the NHL scoring title that season. "Sergei probably came back way too soon," Wharton said. "We just didn't know enough."Baseline neurological testing wasn't even standardized until the early 2000s. And as much head rattling as Kocur and McCarty might have endured in their fight-filled careers, they both seemed immune from concussion-like symptoms. It just wasn't an issue for them, Wharton said.

There was one incident, however, when Wharton didn't need an MRI machine to know that one of his players was in trouble. Defenseman Bob Rouse had just returned to the bench after taking a hard hit, head first, into the boards. Rouse was sitting on the bench awaiting his next shift but kept looking over his left shoulder, almost like a tic.

In those days, once the game started a heavy dark vinyl curtain hung in the entryway from the bench to the tunnel leading to the Detroit dressing room. Rouse kept looking back.

"Rouser, are you OK, Buddy?"

"Yeah, sure, fine," Rouse said.

"Then what are you looking at?"

Rouse took another quick glance over his shoulder.

"I don't know," he said, "but I have no idea what's behind that curtain."

"OK," Wharton said, "You're done."

And Rouse underwent then what was accepted as concussion protocol. Which is a lot different and better these days, thankfully, Wharton said.

———————————————

Maltby spent the better part of his first full year with the Red Wings living in the Pontchartrain Hotel, until he was finally given a roster spot and told to get his own apartment. Early on at the Pontch, when he still didn't know his way around the city very well, Maltby was in desperate need of a haircut and didn't know where to go.

"I asked Johnny Wharton, our trainer, and he recommended a place on the East Side, over by Grosse Pointe, near Morass and Mack," Maltby said.

So he went for a haircut. And met a girl.

For a time after checking out of the hotel, Maltby and goaltender Kevin (Ticker) Hodson shared an apartment in Oakland County. Eventually, Maltby bought a house in Novi, living there for two years while he dated that girl from the East Side. Wendy, the hairdresser. The two eventually married and bought a place of their own in Grosse Pointe. That was in May of 2001, and they've been there ever since, raising their three children.

"I never thought there would be a day when I didn't go back to Hespeler," Maltby said of his hometown—a 2 1/2-hour drive from Detroit. "But the thing is, I love it here. Absolutely love it."

Same goes for his Grind Line mates—Draper, the assistant GM; Kocur, the former assistant coach turned businessman and philanthropist; and McCarty, the mayor of Hockeytown.

"You've got four Canadian boys here," Maltby said, "and I won't speak for the other guys, but I think we all consider ourselves Michiganders. As much as I love Canada, this is home now."

Up Close and Personal

J osh, wake up!'
My brother, Josh Prentice, was a huge fan of the game of hockey. Though he was an ardent Red Wings supporter, he was more a student of the game and extremely passionate about what it meant to his life. He played hockey for more than forty years. He also coached, he watched, he followed the inner workings of the National Hockey League, and he worked in the game as a college equipment manager, retail salesperson, and sales rep for equipment manufacturers.

Photos courtesy of the Prentice family

Josh Prentice

Josh in his final hours with a special
visitor at his bedside.

Sadly, Josh was diagnosed with Stage 4 colon cancer in June of 2022. Just like the way he played the game every shift of his life, he fought a courageous battle against the disease. Unfortunately it cost him his life. Near the end, less than eighteen months later, his wife Emily wanted to allow his friends and family a chance to visit and say their farewells. On Sunday in November, several came to visit their home in Hazel Park. A friend of mine, Monte Laclear, who was a teammate of Josh's, asked if he could bring someone along who might cheer Josh up a bit as he drifted in and out of consciousness. Of course we said yes.

So that afternoon, Monte and his guest arrived, but we were having a difficult time emerging my brother from his deep slumber.

"Josh, wake up! Someone is here to see you."

Nothing.

"Josh, WAKE UP!"

Still nothing.

And then the visitor spoke. Loudly and clearly.

"Josh, it's Darren McCarty from the Detroit Red Wings! WAKE UP!"

And wake up he did, his eyelids rising slightly, and then wide open as he realized who was standing at his bedside. Then, in a soft, hoarse whisper, Josh spoke.

"Holy shit!" he said. And with all the strength his ravaged body could muster, he lifted his right hand off the bed, just enough to extend it toward McCarty's so they could shake hands. Then, almost immediately, Josh fell back to sleep.

Those were the last words my brother spoke. A few hours later, in the early morning of November 13, his final shift ended. Josh Prentice took that one last hurrah, one final everlasting memory with him, thanks to Darren McCarty. Holy shit!

But Darren wasn't done yet. He spent the next hour or so chatting with our friends and family, regaling them with stories, hugging everyone, comforting my mother and Emily. He was an absolute gentleman and forevermore a hero to our family for the time he spent with us in that very somber moment.

A few weeks later, we held a celebration of Josh's magnificent life at the Detroit City Fieldhouse in old City Sports Arena, where Josh and I played many games. Once again, Darren showed up and spent more of his precious time with a massive crowd on hand to honor my brother. He told more stories and did everything in his power to cheer people up and make sure the event was truly a celebration.

All this love and friendship in a time of need for someone Darren never even knew before. To call him our hero doesn't begin to express how much we appreciate what he did for our family, how thankful we are, and how we will never, ever forget his kindness.

Bryan Prentice
Royal Oak, Michigan

#getacolonoscopy
#earlydetection

A Life-Affirming Pep Talk
I was a late bloomer when it came to hockey. I wasn't introduced to the sport until my freshman year in high school. There was this guy in my English class who always wore Red Wings jerseys, and I would tease him with remarks like, "Dead Wings." This was in 1991-92, when fans were actually going crazy for their Wings, who had finally buried their terrible reputation.

More than that, something about that boy's love of hockey and his passion for the Wings appealed to me. We became friends, and his friends, all of them hockey players, became my friends. And through them, I noticed that people all around Michigan were falling in love with Detroit's hockey team. I joined them, and it felt like I was suddenly part of something special. It changed my life forever.

Darren McCarty with Jenn Reed after she received the news that she was cancer-free.

My new friends taught me the game. I attended their games on weekend nights—the high school equivalent of beer-league competition. By the end of my school days, I was strapping on skates and joining them on the ice.

Each year, with my favorite players Chris Osgood and Darren McCarty, the Wings got better and better. We had the talent. We had the coaching. But somehow we always fell just short. Then, the Kris Draper/Claude Lemeiux incident in happened 1966. Business was unfinished. You could feel it coming in the 1996-97 season. Something was going to happen. It had to happen.

And it did. March 26,1997. "Fight Night at The Joe," or, as we commemorate it now, "Turtle Day." I was home from college that night, a Tuesday, and I had just put my baby sister to sleep when I turned on the hockey game. What transpired elevated Darren McCarty to hero status in my book. Not only did he deliver the sweet revenge that every Wings fan so desperately wanted, but he scored the game-winning goal, in overtime!

That game seemed to turn the switch for the Wings. They would not be denied. And in true storybook fashion, DMac scored the Stanley Cup-winning goal. My favorite goal of all time. We finally won a Stanley Cup in Detroit!

I am one of the lucky ones. I grew up with Steve Yzerman, Nicklas Lidstrom, Sergei Fedorov and the Russian Five, and the amazing Grind Line—Kris Draper, Kirk Maltby, Joe Kocur and, later, Darren. I watched them grow into one of the most dominating checking lines in the history of the NHL. My teenage crushes. My heroes.

Fast forward to, well, four Stanley Cup titles later. I was diagnosed with Stage 3A breast cancer in December 2017, and I started six months of chemotherapy the following month. By March, the chemo had started to take a toll on me, both physically and mentally. I was struggling, badly. But on March 18, 2018, I had the opportunity to meet one of my childhood heroes. Darren McCarty was signing autographs at a local restaurant. I decided I needed to be there.

I wasn't feeling the greatest, but I didn't care. I was going. And I'm so glad I did. The moment I walked into the same room as DMac, I forgot that I was sick. He was everything I had hoped he would be: so much great energy, so outgoing, so very kind. But he went far above and beyond just signing his name for me that day. After knowing me for all of thirty seconds, this girl from Grand Rapids who loved hockey and her Red Wings, Darren gave me the pep talk of all pep talks. He talked about how strong I was, about how I was going to beat cancer. And I believed him! He was compassionate, empathetic, and he gave me some of that strength and wisdom that he found when he went through his own dark times.

Fortunately for me, my story didn't end there. I saw DMac again later that fall after I was declared cancer-free, and we celebrated! I shared all my updates after all my checkups, and he would always find truly heartfelt words of support. After six years, I have had many such moments with DMac, each one better than the last.

Somehow, in some surreal way, my hero has become a very dear friend. Through it all, Darren has never changed. He's tenacious, wildly enthusiastic, and always freely sharing of himself and his huge heart with anyone who needs a little piece of it. As often as possible, I watch him skate with the Detroit Red Wings Alumni. He's still got it, always energizing the crowd, having fun, playing the game we both love.

They say you shouldn't meet your childhood heroes, that you'll always come away disappointed. I am living, cancer-free proof that sometimes you should.

Jennifer Reed
Grand Rapids

#BreastCancerAwareness
#BCRCSB

Author's note: If it seems like Darren McCarty is everywhere these days, he is. If it feels like he lives for these kinds of moments, he does. One of Detroit's all-time sports heroes, McCarty is a self-professed man of the people, by the people and for the people. And he wouldn't have it any other way.

"To me, the great connection is to the people. That's what keeps me going," he said. "All this stuff that I do? It's who I am. It's more the Darren in me than the DMac."

Rubbing shoulders with fans in the corridors of Little Caesars Arena, posing with them for selfies, scribbling his name on scraps of paper, and yes, even visiting strangers on their death beds—it is the oxygen that keeps him alive, and maybe sane.

"One million percent," he said. "It's like breathing, and I'm grateful I can do that. I'm a battery, and the people are my power. It's what I truly love. And it helps get me out of myself. I need that to remind me that all the crazy shit that goes on in my head isn't real."

In this and many other ways, Darren McCarty is the unofficial and highly effective ambassador for the Detroit Red Wings. They would be wise to put him on the payroll – and make it official.

Curtain Calls

Successful National Hockey League franchises are no different than any other thriving organizations; they're led by strong, competent people. So it should be a surprise to no one that three of the four Grind Liners continued to work for the Red Wings after their playing days – and the fourth, as noted, is the unofficial point man for the club.

When injuries forced him out of the game in 1999, in the midst of his sixteenth NHL season, Joe Kocur stayed on as a video coordinator under Scotty Bowman, and later as an assistant to Bowman's successor, Dave Lewis. When Kirk Maltby retired in 2010 after sixteen seasons, he moved seamlessly into a pro scouting role. A year later, when Kris Draper reluctantly hung up his skates after a twenty-year NHL career, he stayed on as special assistant to then General Manager Ken Holland.

Darren McCarty, fifty-two, was trying to establish a second career as a rock star while he was still in the prime of his hockey career. Immensely popular among local sports fans, he has continued to pursue myriad interests since the end of his encore performance with Detroit in 2008. Even while he was helping the Wings win three Stanley Cup titles in six seasons, he was spending the off-season as the front man for his band, Grinder. He has dabbled in media, authoring a book, *My Last Fight* with Kevin Allen, starting his own podcast, "Grind Time," and appearing on various local radio stations.

(For the record, I like to think I helped launch his radio career. I had just founded the "Ice Time" show on Detroit's inaugural all-sports station (WDFN AM-1130) on Monday evenings, 6-8 p.m., in September of 1994—just as the NHL was experiencing its first work-stoppage. Owners locked out the players over bitter contract negotiations. A few months later, I was on assignment in Moscow for the *Free Press* while a group of former Soviet hockey stars in the NHL returned to Russia for a series of games during the lockout. I needed substitutes for the radio show while I was away, so I asked two of the best talkers in the Wings' dressing room, Shawn Burr and Darren McCarty, to fill in. (I joined them by phone from Moscow, and both proved to be outstanding hosts.)

McCarty also starred in the ESPN documentary *Unrivaled* with Claude Lemieux in 2022. More recently, McCarty has immersed himself in professional wrestling, both as a participant and a manager. And when we spoke during the summer of 2024, he said he was close to re-launching his own line of cannabis, which he credits for saving his life by helping him overcome his addiction to alcohol. He's a busy guy.

So is Kocur, sixty, who dabbled in the restaurant business with Dave Lewis—Joe and Lewie's Penalty Box in Fenton—when their coaching days ended. Since then, Kocur co-founded his own company, KocuRoss Group, in Auburn Hills. It's a sales and marketing firm representing automotive suppliers. He's also president of the Joe Kocur Children's Foundation, which he created in 2002. And while serving as president of the Detroit Red Wings Alumni Association for more than a decade, Kocur was the honorary co-spokesperson for the Ted Lindsay Foundation.

Kocur credits Lindsay, the late, great Red Wings captain, for helping him to appreciate the importance of giving back. That led to his first charity softball game, which raised tens of thousands of dollars until the Covid pandemic put an end to it. That event was replaced by an annual golf outing—forty foursomes at $2,500 a pop. Do the math. It's impressive. The foundation is all voluntary; no one is paid a penny, and Kocur knows where every dime goes. Kocur's kids are the beneficiaries, and they include special needs children, the Special Olympics and Wings of Mercy, which helps pay for transportation for children who need surgery, and scholarships, he told the *Detroit Free Press*.

Maltby and Draper remain with the club. Maltby, fifty-two, figures he sees about 230 games a season, trying to keep a book on opposing NHL players and teams. Draper, fifty-three, is now an assistant GM and director of amateur scouting for Executive VP and GM Steve Yzerman, which means Draper logs a lot of international miles trying to unearth the best and brightest prospects for the organization. Besides running the club's selection process in the annual NHL Entry Draft, Draper has immersed himself in other aspects of running an NHL club, such as evaluating potential trades, negotiating contracts, and managing the salary cap.

"I've been so fortunate, since Kenny offered me a job, a great opportunity in the front office," said Draper, who was added to staff while Jim Nill was still assistant GM to Holland. Now Nill is running his own very successful team in Dallas. "Two of the classiest men in our sport, and they've been so good to me. I can pick up the phone any time and have a conversation with both Ken and Jim, and that's a luxury that not a lot of hockey people have.

"Now I have the opportunity to work with Stevie Y. Obviously, we accomplished so much together on the ice, I want to accomplish that in the front office with Steve as well."

Like Nill, and more recently Pat Verbeek, who was mentored by Holland and Yzerman before he was hired as GM in Anaheim, it seems like just a matter of time before Draper has his own team. But where? It's something he doesn't allow himself to even think about.

"Right now, I'm all in with the Detroit Red Wings," he said. "I'm all in with Stevie as one of his assistant GMs. That's my mindset. I would also say that like a lot of guys in the industry who are assistants, the goal is to have your own team. That's something I'm going to continue to work hard to do. I was able to play hockey in the NHL for twenty years, and a lot of that came from work ethic, the same work ethic I bring to the front office. I just try to outwork the competition and get my opportunity."

Since Jim Devellano was brought in as general manager in 1982, Wings management and ownership have made smooth succession to critical roles within the organization a priority. They put a lot of emphasis on grooming the right people for the right jobs when they become open. So this prediction is hardly a reach: not necessarily soon, but reasonably within five years or so, Yzerman will step aside and up. He will continue to as the club's final authority as president, but he'll turn the day-do-day operations over to Kris Draper, the next general manager of the Detroit Red Wings.

The Flight Club

One thousand and three men had worn the Detroit hockey sweater in the franchise's ninety-eight-year history entering the 2024-25 season—902 skaters and 101 goaltenders. They had worn eighty-seven different uniform numbers. Just eight of those numbers have been retired to the rafters.

That's fewer than ten percent of the numbers worn, representing less than .008 percent of all those who have played for the Red Wings. Those numbers will inevitably rise in the years ahead when the Wings raise the numbers of a few more recently retired, Hall of Fame-honored players. But certainly there are more players who served the franchise with distinction deserving of some kind of special recognition, eh?

It is time to consider, then, a kind of Red Wings Ring of Honor as a way to acknowledge and cherish them. It doesn't have to be called Ring of Honor, a common title used by myriad teams in hockey and other sports, though I have no problem with it. Maybe "Wings of Honor" works a little better, considering the club's iconic logo. Or, my preference, "The Flight Club" for players who truly earned their wings in Detroit.

Doesn't really matter to me, as long as we do something. Too many players have accomplished too much, bringing honor and prestige to the franchise; they deserve this special kind of merit. That certainly includes guys like Larry Aurie, whose No. 6 was retired by a previous owner but never raised by the Ilitches, and Sergei Fedorov, whose No. 91 would be in the rafters by now if the Ilitches hadn't felt betrayed by his choice to leave Detroit, twice.

At any rate, offered here is at least a partial list—hardly complete but meant merely to begin the conversation—of players (only) to consider for admission into the Detroit Red Wings "Flight Club" in alphabetical order in an effort to avoid any semblance of partiality:

Larry Aurie, No. 6, right wing, 1926-44. The first truly great player in franchise history dating to 1926, when the club was named the Detroit Cougars, then the Detroit Falcons, before becoming the Detroit Red Wings in 1932. Aurie was a dazzling puck-handler, nicknamed "The Little Rag Man" for the way he controlled the puck, especially on the penalty kill. One of the smallest players in the league at 5-foot-6, he was also one of its toughest. Widely considered to be among the best players of his era and worthy of consideration by the Hockey Hall of Fame. Club owner James Norris called him the heart and soul of the Red Wings. Norris also retired the number but never raised it to the rafters. It remains out of service during the Ilitch ownership era.

Pavel Datsyuk, No. 13, center, 2001-16. Nicknamed "The Magic Man," he is a member of the exclusive "Triple Gold Club" winning gold in the Olympics, the World Championships and the NHL's Stanley Cup. Inducted into the Hockey Hall of Fame. Destined to see his No. 13 raised to the rafters at Little Caesars Arena—at least until he deserted the Wings with a year remaining on his contract to continue his career in Russia. Club ownership and management were not amused. Nevertheless, he has earned this recognition.

Kris Draper, No. 33, center, 1993-2011, one of just five men to play 1,000-plus games in a Red Wings uniform. Ninth all-time in NHL history with 222 Stanley Cup playoff games. Four Stanley Cup rings. The centerpiece of the most decorated fourth (checking) line in league history.

Sergei Fedorov, No. 91, center, 1990-2003, arguably the most talented player ever to wear the winged wheel—after Gordie Howe. Fedorov is a former league MVP, two-time Selke Award winner, and a Lester B. Pearson Award winner with three Stanley Cup rings. Inducted into the Hockey Hall of Fame in 2015. A lock to have his number hanging from the rafters . . . until he betrayed the Wings for a second time by signing with Anaheim—for $10 million less than Detroit's best offer in 2003.

Slava Fetisov, No. 2, defenseman, 1994-98, one of the greatest players ever produced by the mighty Soviet Red Army school. Russia's most decorated player ever who completed his impressive war chest by helping Detroit win back-to-back Stanley Cup titles in 1997-98. If only Wings fans could have seen this man in his prime. His skills were breathtaking.

Ebenezer (Ebbie) Goodfellow, No. 15, center/defenseman, 1929-44, helped the Red Wings win the Stanley Cup three times in his career, serving as captain of the Wings for five seasons. Nicknamed "Poker Face," he was the first Red Wing to win the NHL's Hart Trophy as the league's most valuable player. He was inducted into the Hockey Hall of Fame in 1963.

Joe Kocur, No. 26, right wing, 1984-91 and 1996-99, played 505 of his 820 NHL games in Detroit, in two distinct chapters. In the first, he and pal Bob Probert cut a wide swath in NHL rinks to enable captain Steve Yzerman to do his thing. Probert and Kocur rank one-two in franchise history in penalty minutes. In Kocur's return to the Wings in 1996, he brought his beer-league skills to Detroit and scored some of the prettiest goals of his career to help them win the Stanley Cup in 1997 and 1998.

Vladimir Konstantinov, No. 16, defenseman, 1991-97, Vlad the Impaler, Vladinator, or just Vladdie to his legion of fans. He was a dominant, game-controlling, game-*changing* defender who was just approaching the prime of his career when it ended in a limousine crash six days after he helped Detroit to its first Stanley Cup crown in forty-two years. That 1996-97 season, he finished second in Norris Trophy balloting as the league's best defenseman.

Slava Kozlov, No. 13, left wing, 1991-2001, the quietest, yet one of the most productive members of Detroit's iconic Russian Five. He played 607 of his 1,182 NHL games in Detroit, scoring 202 goals among 415 points in the regular season and actually increased his point-per-game production in the postseason. A money player, scoring some of the biggest Stanley Cup playoff goals in the 1990s. Traded in 2001 to Buffalo for Dominik Hasek.

Igor Larionov, No. 8, center, 1995-2000 and 2001-03, widely considered to be among the greatest players in the history of the game. He played 539 of his 921 NHL games with Detroit. But like Fetisov, Larionov's prime years were spent behind the Iron Curtain with the Central Red Army Club. He didn't get to the NHL until he was nearly thirty, and he didn't join the Red Wings until he was almost thirty-five—and still played at an elite level for several years in two stints with the Detroit in which he helped win three Stanley Cup titles.

Reed Larson, No. 28, defenseman, 1976-86, one of the best defensemen in franchise history who had the unfortunate luck of playing during its "Dead Wings" era. Tough, durable, with one of the hardest, heaviest shots the game has ever seen, he scored twenty-plus goals in six seasons and still ranks eleventh in club history with 570 points in 708 games.

Kirk Maltby, No. 18, left wing, 1995-2010, a quiet, unassuming, just-happy-to-be-here kind of guy who became a quiet assassin. One of the best NHL's checking wingers and heaviest hitters throughout his career, Maltby could steamroll opponents, and then sting them even harder with some well-chosen words as he skated away. Attached to the hip with center Kris Draper, the two were among the best penalty-killing pairs in the NHL, formed the nucleus of the Grind Line and each won four Stanley Cup rings.

Darren McCarty, No. 25, right wing, 1993-2004; 2007-09, author of one of the most colorful careers in Detroit sports history. Played 659 of his 758 NHL games with Detroit in two stints. Had a memorable fight, taught us all the difference between a sucker punch and a cold-cock, and scored a couple of memorable goals. Known on Google as a Canadian professional wrestler. Who knew?

Larry Murphy. No. 55, defenseman, 1997-2001, played just five of his 21 NHL seasons with the Red Wings, but they were awfully good seasons. He partnered with fellow Hockey Hall of Famer Nick Lidstrom to form an unrivaled partnership on the blue line that helped Detroit win Stanley Cup titles in 1997-98—to go with the two rings he won with Pittsburgh earlier in the decade. One of the most durable and productive defensemen in league history.

Chris Osgood, No. 30, goaltender, 1993-2001 and 2005-11, with 401 victories, three Stanley Cup titles and two other trips to the Cup Final in seventeen seasons, he belongs in the Hockey Hall of Fame with his number hanging from the rafters at Little Caesars Arena.

Period. End of discussion. The second goalie in league history after Detroit's Terry Sawchuk to win Stanley Cup championships ten years apart (1998-2008). Oh, and he scored a goal, with nineteen assists in 744 NHL games.

Marty Pavelich, No. 11, center, 1947-1957, a fast, defense-minded checker and penalty killer, he was Kris Draper 1.0. Pavelich, who died in June 2024 at the age of 96, helped Detroit win four Stanley Cup titles in the 1950s. In fact, Gordie Howe said frequently that the Wings wouldn't have won any of those championships without Pavelich. That's how important he was to those teams.

Bob Probert, No. 24, left wing, 1985-94, he played just over half of his checkered NHL career in Detroit—but it was the best half. The NHL's all-time greatest fighter, the guy could play hockey, too. In a season in which he logged 398 penalty minutes (nearly seven full games), he also scored twenty-nine goals and earned a spot in the NHL All-Star Game. He could hurt opponents with his fists, but as a hockey player he had Hall of Fame hands.

Marcel Pronovost, No. 3, defenseman, 1950-65, summoned to Detroit during the Stanley Cup playoffs in 1950 after Gordie Howe was injured. HOF defenseman Red Kelly moved to forward to replace Howe, and Pronovost—a defensive defenseman—took his spot and stayed there. The Wings won the Cup that season, and Pronovost helped them win in 1952, '54 and '55. His number also belongs in the rafters at LCA; he was inducted into the Hockey Hall of Fame in 1978.

Mickey Redmond, No. 20, right wing, 1970-76, bingo-bango, could this guy ever shoot the puck! In 1972-73, he became the NHL's seventh player—and first for Detroit—to score fifty goals. He finished with fifty-two and followed it up with fifty-one the next season. Sadly, his career was cut short by chronic back issues. But he remained in the game in the broadcast booth, where he has enjoyed a Hall of Fame career since the mid-1980s alongside the late Dave Strader and Ken Daniels.

Brendan Shanahan, No. 14, left wing, 1996-2006, played just under half of his 1,524 NHL games with the Red Wings, but they included the best and most productive years in his career. He scored 309 goals among 633 points in his 716 games in Detroit, helping his team win three Stanley Cup titles. He was inducted into the Hockey Hall of Fame in 2013.

John (Black Jack) Stewart, No. 2, defenseman, 1938-1950, widely regarded as the hardest-hitting defenseman of his time with a style that resulted in injuries, scars and one of the most colorful nicknames in the game. He once returned to play in the same game he suffered a ruptured disc. In another game, he returned to play despite a fractured skull. He won two Stanley Cups with Detroit and was inducted into the Hockey Hall of Fame in 1964.

Norm Ullman, No. 7, center, 1955-68, one of the most consistent producers—and highest-scoring centers—in NHL history. He played thirteen of his twenty-three NHL seasons in Detroit, scoring 324 goals among 758 points in 875 games with the Wings. An elegant stick-handler and tenacious forechecker, he ranks among the greatest players never to win a Stanley Cup. He was inducted into the Hockey Hall of Fame in 1982.

Mike Vernon, No. 29, goaltender, 1995-1997, he played just ninety-five of his 782 NHL games with the Red Wings, but he made 'em count. In his second season in Detroit, he led the Wings to the Stanley Cup Final. In his third season, he helped them win it all, and in the process earn Conn Smythe Trophy honors as the best

196 / The Grind Line

playoff performer that spring. While he was in Detroit, he mentored goaltending partner Chris Osgood. Vernon was inducted into the Hockey Hall of Fame in 2024.

Henrik Zetterberg, No. 40, center, 2002-18, played his entire fifteen-year career with Detroit, winning a Stanley Cup ring in 2008 and then succeeded Nick Lidstrom as the Wings' captain. Scored 337 goals among 960 points in 1,082 games, and did it with class and distinction. Next stop: the Hockey Hall of Fame.

Potential Auxiliary (non-player nominees) members, limited to coaching, scouts, and front-office execs, to consider: Jack Adams, Hakaan Andersson, Scotty Bowman, Jacques Demers, Jim Devellano, Ken Holland, Dave Lewis, and Barry Smith

Acknowledgements

Memory is the diary that we all carry with us, but for some the ink on those ethereal pages fades all too quickly. It's an innate skill we're born with, rarely 100 percent perfect, and the degree of accuracy in how we remember things can vary from person to person.

Such is the challenge of telling a true, multi-faceted story whose origins date back nearly six decades.

"I can't remember shit, so I don't know how much I can help you," Joe Kocur said as we sat down for an interview over a cold drink in his favorite local saloon. He was a few months shy of his fifty-ninth birthday, and truth be told there were things he recalled with remarkable detail. Other things, not so much. But research helped fill the gaps.

Then there was Scotty Bowman, approaching ninety-one when we visited to discuss the subject of this book. Like the very first conversation we had more than thirty years ago, I came away fascinated by the detail in every anecdote he shared, some of them going as far back as the 1960s. Sharp as an Obsidian blade, as always, a walking contradiction, self-styled and unapologetic, with the heart of a lion. I am deeply indebted to Scotty for his willingness to write the foreword to this book about what I know now are some of his favorite players.

Same goes for Jim Devellano, eighty-one, the architect of the modern-day Detroit hockey dynasty and a self-described historian of the National Hockey League. In the forty years I've known him, he's never refused an interview, never ducked a tough question, never passed up an opportunity to help educate me about the game, the league, or his Detroit Red Wings. And he did so with absolutely brilliant detail right down to recalling certain conversations verbatim.

Such was the joy of putting this book together, spending time with all the principle subjects whose careers I covered as a beat writer and columnist for the *Detroit Free Press*—Kocur, Kris Draper, Kirk Maltby and Darren McCarty—and reliving through them some of the best moments in the history of this century-old franchise. Among the other dozens of interviews over the years that helped to inspire this book, I am especially indebted to Scotty Bowman (who graciously agreed to pen the foreward to this book), Jim Devellano, Ken Holland, Doug MacLean, Dave Lewis, Mike Modano, the late Bob Probert, Brendan Shanahan, John Wharton and Steve Yzerman for sharing their experiences relating to the Grind Line with me.

Original reporting in the form of first-person interviews, while absolutely critical, only go so far. Where memory's potholes failed Kocur, the outstanding book he and Probert wrote with Windsor author Bob Duff, *The Bruise Brothers* was invaluable. So was McCarty's brutally honest book, *My Last Fight*, written with Kevin Allen. And MacLean's *Draft Day*, written with Scott Morrison. They were valuable resources, and I highly recommend them all. Chronicles in newspapers, including the *Detroit Free Press, Detroit News, Oakland Press, MLive,* the *Toronto Sun,* and websites like *DetroitHockeyNow.com, HockeyDB.com, ThePlayersTribune.com,* among others, were vital in tracking down facts and harvesting truth from gossip and innuendo. My profound gratitude to these and other sources. Meantime, any errors here are mine alone.

I am beyond proud to showcase the work of graphic artist Josh Chamberlain, who designed the cover of this book. He was one of my many talented students during my years as adviser to *The Washtenaw Voice*, the nationally honored student newspaper at Washtenaw Community College. To Ryan Sprenger and Tim Boddenberg at Printopya Publishing, my profound gratitude for your guidance—and patience.

My thanks, as well, to Red Wings fans, many of whom confirmed without reservation that the Grind Line was a worthy subject for a book and to others who were kind enough to share their inspiring stories of close encounters with the members of that special unit. Bryan Prentice and Jennifer Reed, and several others were kind enough to share their experiences. Thanks especially to Sue Lefever of the 75-year-old For'Em (Win or Lose) Club, the oldest NHL team fan club, for connecting me to those fans.

I have been the beneficiary of nearly four decades of masterful work by the Red Wings' public relations and marketing staff—starting with Bill Jamieson (the Wayne Gretzky of PR men) in the mid-1980s through Todd Beam today. Their efforts made life a lot easier for all of us charged with covering a major professional franchise in a sports-rabid town like Detroit.

This feels like a good time to acknowledge those who read my previous books and offered not just occasional praise but helpful, constructive criticism that gave me the kind of confidence to keep The Russian Five from being a one-off. Thanks to them and to all good readers of books.

My deepest thanks to my wife, Jo Ann, for putting up with a cranky recluse who spent his late summer weeks trying to meet a publishing deadline while she did most of the heavy lifting—

housetraining the latest addition to our family, a golden retriever puppy, Garp.

Finally, a sincere apology to those deserving souls I've failed to mention in this space. The only reasonable excuse I can offer: I have a lousy memory.

Index

Buffalo Ankerites, 22
Buffalo Sabres, 18, 127, 192
Bure, Pavel, 73, 75
Burr, Shawn, 174, 186
Buyck, Johnny, 20
Buffalo Sabres, 16, 18, 148

Calgary, 73
Calgary Flames, 50
Cambridge, Ontario, 89
Cambridge Winter Hawks, 93
Campbell, Colin, 126-127
Canadian Football League, 117
Canadian Tire, 89
Cape Breton, Nova Scotia, 97
Cape Breton Oilers, 99
Carnegie, Herb, 22
Carnegie, Ossi, 22
Carolina Hurricanes, 148
Century Line, 20
Chamberlain, Josh, 199
Charron, Guy, 73, 79
Chase, Kelly, 115, 156
Chelios, Chris, 86, 160
Cherry, Don, 23
Cheveldae, Tim, 61
Chicago, 80
Chicago Blackhawks, 18, 110-113
Ciccarelli, Dino, 108
City Sports Arena (Detroit), 179
Cizikas, Casey, 23
Clark, Jim, 62-63, 84

Lemieux, Mario, 20, 167
Lester B. Pearson Award, 191
Lewis, Brenda, 40
Lewis, Dave, 41, 54, 59, 88, 106, 108, 131, 151-155, 164, 169-170, 185, 196, 198
Lidstrom, Nicklas, 12, 58, 86, 100, 138, 143, 152, 181, 193
LILCO Line, 16
Lindros, Eric, 18, 24, 49, 104, 143-144, 173
Lindsay, Ted, 17-18, 25
Little Caesars Arena, 26, 183, 190, 193
Little Caesars pizza, 125
Little League Baseball, 34
London, Ontario, 57
Long Island Lighting Company, 16
Los Angeles Kings, 16, 18, 123, 168-169
Low, Ron, 99

McCreary, Bill, 104
MacDonald, Lowell, 20
MacInnis, Al, 86, 135
MacLean, Doug, 33, 41-42, 55-64, 68, 77, 84, 151, 153
MacLean, Jill, 55
Mafia Line, 21
Mahon, Jim, Memorial Trophy, 30
Mahovlich, Frank, 18, 21
Maine (AHL), 122
Makarov, Sergei, 22, 27, 79
Maloney, Don, 21
Maltby, Kirk, 12-14, 24, 26-28, 46-48, 52, 61, 85-104, 128, 135, 138-139, 142, 144, 152, 160-161, 164, 166, 169-172, 175, 181, 185, 187, 192, 198
Maltby, Ella, 91

Nieuwendyk, Joe, 135, 148
Niinamaa, Janne, 48, 139
Nill, Jim, 187
Norris, James, 190
Norris Trophy, 192
Northeastern University, 61, 98
Novi, Michigan, 175
Nowinski, Chris, 173

Oakland County, 175
Oakland Hills Country Club, 69, 105, 107
Oakland Press, 198
Oak Park Ice Arena, 167
Oates, Adam, 124
Olympic Winter Games, 1992, 73
Ontario, 22, 32
Ontario Hockey League, 30, 40, 72, 75, 94-95, 100, 119
Osgood, Chris, 30, 60, 166, 180, 193, 195
Ottawa Senators, 58, 170
Ottawa 67s, 30, 34, 75
Owen Sound, Ontario, 95
Owen Sound Platers, 87

Paddock, John, 63
Pan American Games, 116
Park, Brad, 124-125
Parrish, Lance, 34
Pastrnak, David, 21-22
Patrick, Craig, 21
Pavelich, Mark, 20
Marty Pavelich, 153, 191
Pelly Gerald, 92